sno[w]

les

paradiski

first edition 2004

written and edited by
Michael Kayson & Isobel Rostron

Qanuk Publishing & Design Ltd
www.snowmole.com

the snowmole guide to **les arcs paradiski**
first edition 2004

published by Qanuk Publishing & Design Ltd
45 Mysore Road London SW11 5RY

copyright © Qanuk Publishing & Design Ltd 2004
maps © Qanuk Publishing & Design Ltd 2004
artwork © oliver brodrick-ward 2003

printed by Craftprint, Singapore

ISBN 0-9545739-7-8

A catalogue record of this book is available from the British Library.

contents

how to use the guide

How much you enjoy your winter holiday depends on a variety of things. Some you cannot influence - you can't guarantee sunshine, good snow, or your flight landing on time... but most things should be within your control. With the majority of ski holidays lasting just a week or less, you don't want to waste time trying to find a good restaurant, or struggling with an overgrown piste map. The snowmole guides are designed with 2 purposes in mind: to save you time by providing essential information on the operation of the resort, and to help you to make the most of your time by giving insight into every aspect of your stay.

The guide is not intended to be read from cover to cover. After the introduction to the resorts, the guide is split into 4 distinct sections - getting started, the skiing, the resorts and the a-z - so you can dip into the information you need when you need it. Some information will be useful to you beforehand, some while you are in resort and some while you are on the mountain.

getting started   deals with the basics: how to get to the resorts, how to get around once you're there, and your options when buying your lift pass, renting equipment and booking lessons or mountain guides.

the skiing   gives an overview of the mountains and the ski area, information on the off-piste, and a breakdown for beginners, intermediates, experts, boarders and non-skiers. The ski domain has been divided into digestible chunks and for each there is a detailed description of the pistes and lifts.

the resorts   covers the best of the rest of your holiday: for each of the resorts, there is a series of reviews on where to eat and where to play as well as general sections on what to do when skiing isn't an option, facilities for children and tips for seasonnaires.

the a-z   comprises a list of tour operators, a directory of contact details (telephone numbers and website addresses) and information from accidents to weather, a glossary of terms used in this guide and in skiing in general, and an index to help navigate your way around the guide.

how to use the maps

The guide also features a number of maps, designed and produced specifically for snowmole. While the information they contain is as accurate as possible, some omissions have been made for the sake of clarity.

route maps   show the journey to the resort from the UK, from relevant airports or the roads within the area surrounding the resorts.

resort maps   one for each resort (showing pedestrianised zones, main buildings, and where relevant, car parks, train lines, and road names).

ski maps   each individual area has its own contoured map. These show details such as the lifts, pistes and mountain restaurants. The contours have been mapped to fit an A6 page - few ski areas are perfect rectangles. They are accurate only in relation to the pistes they depict and should not be used for navigation. Pistes are shown only in their approximate path - to make the maps as user-friendly as possible some twists and turns have been omitted. The ski maps are grouped together at the back of the book to make them easy to find and refer to - even with gloves on. There is an overview map on the inside back cover that shows the entire ski domain and how the individual ski maps fit together. The back cover has a flap, which is useful as a page marker for the individual ski maps. In the chapter on the skiing the overview map is reproduced in miniature alongside the descriptions of the individual sectors.

explanation of icons

review headers

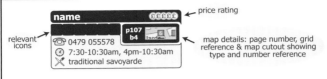

name — price rating

relevant icons

☎ 0479 055578
🕐 7:30-10:30am, 4pm-10:30am
✗ traditional savoyarde

p107
b4

map details: page number, grid reference & map cutout showing type and number reference

basic details

🕿 - telephone number
📠 - fax number
@ - email address
w^3 - website address
🛏 - number of beds
🖃 - office address
🕐 - opening hours
✗ - food type

ski school icons

⛷ - ski lessons
🏂 - snowboard lessons
👫 - child-specific lessons
♿ - disabled skiing
🎿 - specialist courses
G - guides available

hotel icons

🥾 - on-site rental store
🚌 - shuttle bus

others

✗ - food available
🍴→ - take away
♫ - live music
📺 - tv
🖱 - internet station(s)
🍸 - bar
• - terrace

town maps

buildings

ℹ - tourist office
🎿 - lift pass office
PO - post office
🛒 - supermarket
🎬 - cinema
⛪ - church

travel specific

P - parking
🅿 - covered parking
ⓑ - bus stop
🚌 - route specific bus stop

commerce colour coding

■ - savoyarde restaurant
■ - restaurant
■ - cafe
■ - take-away
■ - bar
■ - nightclub
■ - hotel

route maps

 - train line & station

 - main road & town

 - country borders

 - motorway & town

 - airport

 graphic design by Qanuk Publishing & Design Ltd

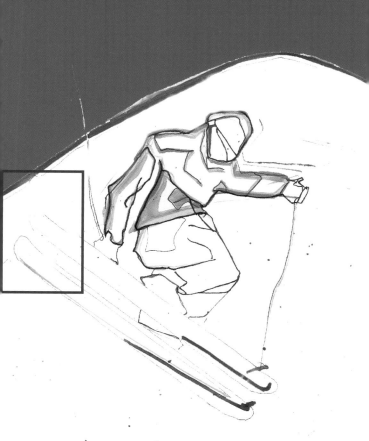

introducing les arcs

In between the self-interested step-sisters of the 3 Vallées and the Espace Killy, and newly wed to its moneyed Prince Charming La Plagne, Les Arcs is very much the Alpine Cinderella. Until recently it had a medium-sized ski area and a marketing budget to match, and the glitzy side of ski-tourism had overlooked the twin peaks of the Grive and Rouge - but all that is set to change. Paradiski's Vanoise Express and the newly developing Arc 1950 are bringing a modern and more upmarket profile to a resort which in places can feel a little tired or outdated - or indeed rather too full of schoolchildren. The skiing is excellent for every ability level even without the La Plagne link, and though you won't find showiness or shopping

to match Courchevel or Val d'Isère, all but the very top end of the market is now catered for. Once you've been, you'll find it difficult not to go back.

Each of Les Arcs' resorts has a very different personality. The main resorts (1800, 1600 and 2000) are all a product of an initial commercial desire to house as many people as possible on the mountain, and as such consist of eyesore apartments and functional walkways, with the odd hotel thrown in for balance. More recent developments like the chalet complexes in Le Chantel or just below Arc 2000 provide some aesthetically pleasing accommodation, and Arc 1950 - though still in its infancy - is designed for a more discerning audience than was anticipated back in the 1960s.

An interesting cross-section of the skiing community make Les Arcs their destination of choice. The plethora of self-catering apartments mean the holidays see hordes of youngsters, either with families or on school trips. As with La Plagne, it is predominantly French in make-up, and alongside a healthy and growing English market Les Arcs also draws a strong Belgian contingent, plus some ambassadors from Holland and Germany.

The majority of the 30,000 beds in Les Arcs are in self-catering apartments. Most of these are pretty standard - there is a lot more functionality and convenience than there is luxury. None of it is very exciting to look at, with the exception of the new wonderland that is Arc 1950. Around the corner in Peisey-Vallandry everything is a little less blocky, with the 10,000 or so beds consisting of a more typical blend of chalets and hotels.

Where you stay will have an enormous effect on the party side of your holiday. Each resort has at least one good spot, but outside of 1800 you will find yourself somewhat short of variety. The jolliest après is to be found in Vallandry, the most English in 1800 and the latest (and the oddest) in 1600. Quiet weeks can be very quiet regardless of which resort you are in - though of all the resorts, Arc 2000 is the least likely to satisfy the hardcore party people. The limited range of an unfinished (and hence under-populated) 1950 is extended for winter 2004, with the opening of a nightclub which will bring closing times in line with the other resorts.

11

snapshot

highs...
tree-skiing above vallandry
excellent network of pistes
great off-piste
the chalets de l'arc mountain restaurant
ideal for families and school trips

and lows
lots of school trips
limited après outside arc 1800
unattractive architecture
limited non-skiing activities
few good restaurants

With a few notable exceptions, eating out in Les Arcs is a pretty dull pastime. Families and school trips are perfectly catered for, with endless inexpensive Savoyarde spots which are all a bit samey - but equally if you know where you're going you can find some superb and very individual restaurants. And the joy of Les Arcs is that even in the best places you can get 3 or 4 courses for the price of 1 in Courchevel. The operative word is convenience, but if you're prepared to go a little out of your way you can also find some top-notch food - and atmosphere to match.

The native ski area is superb but often overlooked by those who are concerned that they get the full range of holiday experiences on their break. Though it may not be the best après destination in the Alps, you can't really fault the skiing, which has the full range of pisted options, some long and exhausting bump runs, a good quality snowpark and an off piste domain to die for. Add the Vanoise Express and you have in Paradiski a complement of options at which the mind boggles.

overview

1800 is the largest, most diverse, most central, and - notwithstanding Arc 1950 the king in waiting - the nicest of the resorts. The purpose-built, apartment block architecture of the main resorts is very much in evidence, and at first sight 1800 is neither attractive nor interesting. The bland wooden façades house a lot of bland commerce, but this is balanced by some splendid surprises. The skiing above the resort is superb, and 1800 also provides the best access to the rest of the area and it also hosts the majority share of the après scene.

1600 is the least English of all the resorts, and also the lowest, the least well appointed and the most immediately unattractive - but for all that it is the most easily accessible. The local skiing is a tad limited and linkage to the rest of the area is unremarkable. 1600's redeeming factor is the funicular link with Bourg St. Maurice providing an escape when you need it.

On a small plateau just a couple of turns past Arc 1950 sits big brother **arc 2000**, the highest of the resorts. Much the same size as 1600 and just as unappealing to look at, 2000's biggest attraction is its altitude - and hence good snow record. Club Med has a significant presence, as do a number of the English high-street tour operators, who run an enclave of pseudo-chalet accommodation that promotes a very British atmosphere.

arc 1950 puts the 'pose' into purpose built. Opened in December 2003 and due for completion by winter 2008, much of the resort is still under construction - but the existing quality of service and attention to detail shows that Arc 1950 is already far and away the best choice for the discerning holidaymaker. Depending on your disposition it is either small and charming or cute and kitschy, either comfortable and classy or expensive and half-finished - but no matter what your first impression, there is no denying that it caters for a market that would otherwise overlook Les Arcs as a destination.

In the trees around the corner from 1800 is an area that has almost nothing in common with the rest of Les Arcs. Not commercial, not full of apartment blocks, and not so subject to holiday over-population, the small communities of **vallandry** and **plan-peisey** are even accessed by a completely different road, governed by a different tourist office and given a collective name: Peisey-Vallandry. Though they share the same ski area, in most other senses they are a world apart. Vallandry is charming and unassumingly friendly - and though Plan-Peisey now has an enormous cable car right in the middle of it, the majority of La Plagne day-trippers head straight off up the hill, leaving intact much of the small town feel.

12

Predicting weather in the mountains is always difficult. Sunny blue skies can become a complete white-out within an hour, and equally a cloudy snowy morning can often become a sunny afternoon of perfect powder. Les Arcs is no exception to this - though with only 1 main ridge line there are rarely separate conditions between the areas. If you can't see the Grive from Arc 2000, you probably can't see it from the Vanoise Express either, and similarly if it's sunny all day on the terrace of the Chalets de l'Arc, it's probably equally sunny at the Blanc in Vallandry.

temperatures

It's fairly easy to generalise temperatures - December and January are usually the coldest months, with things warming up gradually through February, March and April. Temperatures can range from -15°C at ground level on the coldest days to as high as 20°C later on in the season when the sun is shining.

13

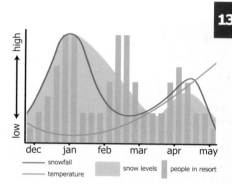

snowfall
temperature

snow levels — people in resort

snowfall

When and how much snow falls varies from year to year, but general trends do emerge. Les Arcs is very standard as regards snowfall and season length. There's nothing particularly high up, and nothing too low down - 1600 is most prone to slush, along with the bottom end of the Villaroger sector, and 1800 can get thin by early April if it's warm.

volume of people in resort

As you might expect from a resort that is popular with schools and families, the population varies dramatically from week to week. In the holidays it is jammed, and in the off-peak weeks it fluctuates from busy-ish to completely dead, both in resort and on the slopes. The seasonnaire population isn't huge, totalling about 450 across the resorts, but it is enough to give it at least some life in quiet weeks - particularly in 1800 and Vallandry.

Ski resorts are as varied as DNA. But what makes Les Arcs Les Arcs? For a quintessential time...

learn to cook

Holidays are supposed to be about relaxing, unwinding and paying money so that

other people do things for you. But 'chilling out' on a ski holiday has a slightly different meaning, and the chances are that you'll be getting plenty of exercise during the day. If you're in self-catering accommodation at least one of your party is likely to get a workout in the evening too - you're fending for yourself, so make sure you pack your copy of Delia. Unless you're a fan of take-away pizza.

take a moonlit walk

In winter, the journey between Arc 1800 and Vallandry takes about an hour by car. Walking, it takes a little over 20 minutes up/down the Forêt piste (though your mileage may vary). If you're staying in Vallandry and fancy a different selection of bars and restaurants, or a night that lasts after 1am, make your pedestrian way up to 1800 for the evening. The journey is of course also possible for those in 1800 coming down - but getting

home after a couple of beers is easier going downhill than up.

queue for the rouge

The lift system in general is pretty efficient, and mostly you shouldn't have to wait in line too long wherever you are. There is one exception to this, however - the queues for the Aiguille Rouge cable car above Arc 2000 are seemingly permanent. Even in weeks when it's quiet in resort it is busy at the top of the Varet. And don't be fooled by quiet pistes either - if there's no one where you are, it's probably because they're already standing in line.

try the link

Though the skiing in Les Arcs is very good, and quite extensive enough to keep you happy for a week, these days you have the option of nipping over to La

Plagne for a bit of a change of scene. Once you get there you've got plenty of time on lifts before you do any skiing, but even if you just go over for a bite to eat at the Sauget or on the terrace of the Ferme du Cesar, you can say you've done it. Why bother? Because it's there.

get lost in the woods

The forests above Vallandry are both a safe(ish) place to learn the trade and a superb place to hone your tree-skiing skills. If you've never tried it before there are various obvious lines that leave the piste and wind past a trunk or two before getting you back on safe snow - and experts can pretty much just disappear anywhere, as the trees never get too thick and the terrain never gets too steep. Unless you have a terrible sense of direction you'll never get far from a piste on the way down - and if

you do drop too low, there's a hilarious lift up from Le Villaret that will restore you to Plan-Peisey next to the Vanoise Express.

see what all the fuss is about

The posh new resort just below Arc 2000 exerts a curious draw on those who aren't staying there. In the space of not very long there has appeared a cluster of new and not-unattractive buildings that stick out of the landscape like a not-sore thumb. Most of Les Arcs' accommodation is more high-rise than high-quality - and most of the commerce would fit into a similar word-play about restaurants. There may not (yet) be much of Arc 1950 to see, but what is there is worth the seeing.

break the limit

Skiing attracts all sorts, and Les Arcs' pistes cater pretty well for most of them. Beginners have various designated areas to keep them safe from the traffic, families will enjoy the inexhaustible supply of blues and reds, experts have powder and moguls aplenty. But what, you ask, of the boy racers? Where should they go? To the Kilometre Lancé, of course (➥ activities & events).

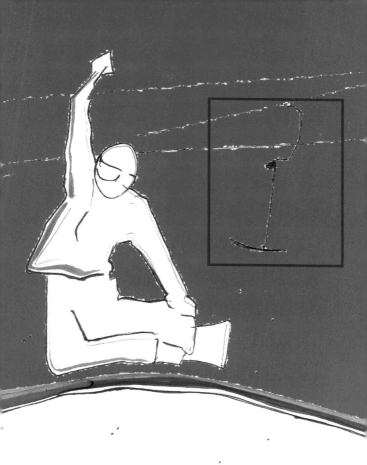

getting started

planning your trip

Once you know you want to go to Les Arcs, you need to decide how you want to get there. Traditionally, most skiing holidays are booked though travel agents or tour operators, but with the advent of cheap flights, DIY holidays are becoming more popular. There are pros and cons to both.

18 package

The theory behind package holidays is that all you should have to think about is getting from the top of the slopes to the bottom. The core of every package deal is convenience - though it comes wrapped in all kinds of paper. Ski companies fall into 2 types: large mainstream operators, and smaller more specialist ones. The mainstream brand offers ready-made holidays, where everything is already planned and you take it or leave it. Trips with smaller companies can be more expensive, but tend to be more flexible and many tailor the trip to your exact requirements. Alternatively, if you don't want to be restricted to a single operator, a travel agent will have access to a selection of holidays offered by several companies.

Mainstream companies only run week-long trips, from Saturday to Saturday or Sunday to Sunday - giving you 6 days on the slopes and 7 nights in (or on) the town. They charter their own **flights** - making the holiday cheaper - but you have little option as to when or from where you travel. Smaller ski

companies give you greater choice - many specialise in long weekends for the 'money-rich, time-poor' market, with departures on Thursday evenings and returns on Monday evenings. This gives you 4 days skiing for 2 days off work... but the real advantage is their use of scheduled flights, so you can pick the airport, airline, and when you travel.

With a mainstream company, your **transfer** to resort will be by coach, with others who have booked through the same company. You may have to wait for other flights, and on the way there may be stop-offs in other resorts or at other accommodation before your own. Because you're travelling at the weekend the journey tends to take longer. With a smaller company you may transfer by coach, minibus, taxi, or car depending on how much you've paid and the size of your group. And if you arrive mid-week, the transfers tend to be quicker.

What your **accommodation** is depends entirely on whom you book with. Some companies only offer apartments, some specialise in chalets, some operate in specific resorts... the limiting factor is what's in the brochure - though if you want to stay in a particular place, a more specialist company may try to organise it for you.

In **resort** the main benefit of a package holiday is the resort rep. From the moment you arrive to the moment you leave, there is someone whose job it is to ensure your holiday goes smoothly... or that's the theory. More than likely your rep will sort out lift passes and equipment rental. Some will organise evening activities and be available for a short period every day to answer questions. Most are supported by an in-situ manager who deals with more serious issues. The more you pay for your holiday, the better your rep should be. The best are service-oriented French speakers... but it is difficult to recruit hard-working, intelligent, bilingual people to work for next to nothing. If you want to know what - or who - to expect, ask when you book.

DIY

If you DIY, you have more control over the kind of holiday you take and what you pay. But as you have to make all the arrangements, you'll need more time to plan the trip.

Several **airports** are within transfer distance of Les Arcs - so you can fly to whichever one has the most convenient flights for you. The major airports are Geneva and Lyon St. Exupéry, which are serviced by the major airlines (BA, Air France or Swiss) as well as some of the budget options (such as Easyjet and bmibaby). Some of the budget airlines also fly to the smaller airports of St. Etienne, Chambéry and Grenoble. The cheapest flights are normally from London, and the earlier you book the cheaper it will be. The airlines accept

reservations for the upcoming winter from around June or July. Some chartered airlines such as Monarch or Thomas Cook may also have a limited number of seats for sale. For **transfers** to Les Arcs you have a variety of options (➡ getting there). If you don't want to fly, the excellent European motorway system makes **driving** to the Alps surprisingly easy. Getting there by **train** is also an option.

19

On a DIY trip the choice of **accommodation** is endless - you are not restricted by brochures or company deals... however the easiest way to book a chalet or an apartment is through a company or website offering accommodation only, such as Interhome or ifyouski.com. You can liaise with the owners directly if you can find their details, but this is often difficult. For hotels you might be able to get a discount off the published price by contacting them directly. For more information on hotels, chalets and apartments ➡ accommodation.

In **resort** is perhaps where the difference between DIY and package is most noticeable. There is no rep on hand so you have to buy your own lift pass, organise your own equipment rental... but this can have its pluses: you can be sure that you get exactly the right type of pass and you can choose which rental shop you use.

The road to Les Arcs is a road much travelled - along with being the route to Paradiski it also leads to the 3 Vallées and the Espace Killy. As such it can be a bit of a slog on transfer day, particularly making your way through Albertville, which needs a bypass road like you need your mobile phone. The road up from Bourg St. Maurice is actually very good, inasmuch as it isn't very windy nor particularly long - without traffic it's only about 20 minutes to Arc 1800. Those heading to Peisey-Vallandry take a different road, leaving the route shortly after the town of Aime. It's twisty and narrow in places, but there is substantially less traffic on it and it's a far shorter trip.

20

All contact details for the transport listed can be found in the directory.

overland

The most common starting place for any journey by **car** to the Alps is Calais. You can reach Calais from the UK by the **eurotunnel** or **ferry**. Then by car it is just under 1000kms to Les Arcs - a journey that can be done in 11 hours or less. The journey from Calais takes you east of Paris, through Reims to Dijon, then down past Bourg-en-Bresse. Around Lyon you head east towards Moûtiers, then on to Bourg St. Maurice and up to your resort. There are 2 *péage* (toll) stops on the route south through France, for which you collect a ticket as you enter the motorway and hand it in as you leave. Expect to pay

around €50 in total - you can pay with cash or by credit card.

There are 2 alternatives to the standard **ferry** crossing to Calais. The first is with Norfolkline to Dunkirk - often quieter (and less prone to lorry strikes!) than the Calais services. The second is SpeedFerries.com - a new fast ferry service to Boulogne. SpeedFerries sells tickets on a similar basis to the budget airlines - the earlier you buy, the less you pay.

Eurolines runs **coach** services from the UK to Bourg St. Maurice, from where you can transfer up to the resorts. Once you get to Bourg, your trip is as good as sorted. While all those headed for Val d'Isère hang around looking despondent and waiting for coaches to pick them up, you can just nip over to the funicular and shoot up to Arc 1600. The journey takes all of 7½ minutes - and services run 7:30am-7:30pm. There is a regular bus link between 1600 and all of the other Les Arcs resorts. Alternatively you can catch a bus from the train station in Bourg, which stops in all the resorts. On average it takes an hour to get from Bourg to the last stop - Arc 2000. The service runs frequently throughout the day, 7am-midnight - book through the *centrale de réservation* (t 0479 076800, i lesarcs.com).

Travelling **by train** to this part of the Alps gives you more time in resort - 8

fly-drive p.23

getting there

days instead of the usual 6 - a particularly excellent service if you live in London. The stop for Les Arcs is Bourg St. Maurice. As for long distance coach travel, once you're in Bourg you can just hop on the funicular. All train services from the UK become full months in advance so be sure to book well ahead - tickets are released for sale in the July before the start of the season. The **snowtrain** is the classic way to travel by train to the Alps. You check in at Dover on Friday afternoon, take a ferry to Calais where you board a couchette (a train with sleeping compartments) and travel overnight, arriving in the Alps on Saturday morning. The return service leaves the following Saturday evening.

Another option is the **eurostar overnight** service, which leaves London Waterloo (with some services stopping in Ashford, Kent) on Friday evenings. You travel directly to Paris, where you change onto a couchette to travel overnight. As with the snowtrain you arrive in the Alps on Saturday morning and return on Saturday evening. The **eurostar direct** service runs during the daytime, leaving London Waterloo on Saturday mornings and arrives in the Alps on Saturday evenings. The return trip departs on Saturday evening.

If you can't get onto the Eurostar services, the French **intercity** service is an option, a journey that is best started in Paris. The journey to Bourg takes around 5 hours. To get to Paris, you can either fly or take the Eurostar. The transfer from Bourg is the same as for overland coach travel.

by air

Lyon St. Exupéry (205kms) and Geneva (160kms) are the 2 closest international airports to Les Arcs - the greatest number of flights are to Geneva. There are less frequent air services to Lyon St. Etienne (280kms), Grenoble (185kms) and Chambéry (125kms).

transfers

The standard transfer time from Geneva or Lyon is 3-3½ hours. By **car** and with a clear road, this is more like 2½ hours, and conversely on a coach and with Saturday traffic you'll be lucky to make it in fewer than 4. The journey takes you through Albertville and Bourg St. Maurice, either of which would benefit from a failed Swampy protest and a

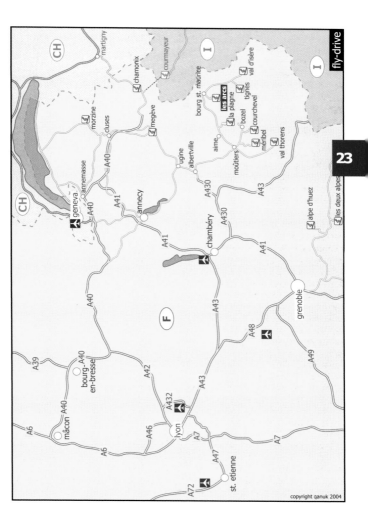

CH

CH

F

I

I

martigny

courmayeur

chamonix

morzine

cluses

megève

bourg st. maurice

les arcs

val d'isère

tignes

la plagne

bozel

courchevel

méribel

val thorens

aime

moûtiers

annemasse

geneva

annecy

ugine

albertville

A40

A41

A40

A41

A430

A43

chambéry

A430

A43

A41

grenoble

A41

A48

alpe d'huez

les deux alpes

A49

bourg-en-bresse

A40

A42

A40

A39

mâcon

A40

A6

A46

A432

lyon

A7

A43

A6

A47

st. etienne

A72

A7

copyright qanuk 2004

bypass. You can hire a car at any of the airports - book over the phone, on the internet, or when you arrive at the airport. Your car will have the necessary equipment such as an emergency triangle, but you will need to specifically ask for snow chains and a roof box if you want them.

24 From Lyon, Grenoble and Chambéry you can get to Les Arcs easily by **train** - there is no direct service from Geneva, which makes it a more tiresome option.

If you don't want to have to worry about driving yourself, there are a number of companies which run **private minibus transfers** from the airport direct to your accommodation. Services vary from a simple pick up and drop off to the provision of welcome packs and food and even champagne during your trip. All of them take online bookings, either via email or direct through the relevant website. ATS run shuttles from Geneva. Most of Alp Line's services run from Geneva though they will pick up from any of the French airports (though this costs more). Mountain Transfers pick up from Geneva, Chambéry and Lyon St. Exupéry and also Bourg St. Maurice. Alpine Cab is the luxury option picking up from Geneva, Grenoble and both Lyon airports. If you don't want to share your personal space with anybody else you can always take a **taxi** - though the privilege of doing so isn't cheap.

As you come up the hill into Les Arcs the first thing you see is quite the worst view you are likely to experience throughout your stay. The front of the Versant Sud résidence in Arc 1600 is unpleasant to say the least - but at least when you see it you're nearly there. It signals the turn off for Arc 1800, and those heading on round to Arc 1950 or 2000 only have another 15 minutes or so if the road is clear.

Once you're there, all you need to get around the resorts is a pair of **feet**. 1800 is about 15 minutes long, as is the road between Plan-Peisey and Vallandry, but you will barely burn a calorie negotiating the other resorts. And they are as simple as they are small - though sometimes in 1800 you may need to take a moment to get your bearings, generally speaking you will have difficulty getting lost.

If you want to try your luck in a different resort, or fancy popping down to Bourg St. Maurice for a spot of shopping, all the resorts are linked to 1600 by **bus** (except Peisey-Vallandry). The service is designed to get people to and from the funicular in 1600, so should you want to get between 1800 and either 1950 or 2000 you will have to change. Buses run approximately every 20 minutes between 7am-7pm.

snapshot

from bourg st. maurice by road to
val d'isère 40 minutes
tignes 40 minutes
st foy 30 minutes
les arcs (by funicular) 7 minutes
les arcs (driving) 20 minutes
les arcs (vallandry) 25 minutes
les arcs (villaroger) 15 minutes
la plagne (montchavin) 20 minutes
la rosière 25 minutes

accommodation

At the end of the day on the slopes, you probably won't mind where you rest your head. But when planning your holiday, you might want to put more thought into where you stay.

With over 40,000 beds between the resorts and plenty of new accommodation on the way, you have ample choice about where to lay your hat in Les Arcs. You are rather more limited, however, in the variety of what you can choose. As a general rule of thumb, accommodation is available in any colour as long as it's a self-catering apartment. There are nice ones and there are not so nice ones. There are also hotels, though not many, and there are chalets and some 'chalet-style' accommodation - most of the genuine chalet accommodation is in Peisey-Vallandry. Outside of low season, last-minute bookings are likely to be relatively difficult to make, but the number of beds in the valley means you are likely to find something somewhere - if you are determined enough to spend a day by the phone. Accommodation can be booked direct or through the tourist office, either by telephone or on their website. Peisey-Vallandry has a separate tourist office and hence a separate website - or for an English run service contact Plan Peisey Accommodation (t 0479 079277, i plan-peisey-accommodation.co.uk), who offer a commission-free accommodation finding service.

hotels

Beggars can't be choosers, and nor can those (no matter what their finances) who want to stay in hotels in Les Arcs. Generally there is very little character and very little of note. With such a limited range you are constricted by either the level of luxury you want or the resort you want to stay in. Your choice is restricted to 3 in 1600, 4 in 1800, 4 in 2000 (of which 2 are Club-Med) and 3 in Peisey-Vallandry. If you want a broader selection, you will need to be prepared to stay away from the ski area - down the hill in Bourg St. Maurice, or below Vallandry in Peisey. The best of those in the ski resorts are La Cachette in 1600 and the Hôtel du Golf in 1800.

specifics

Only the Peisey-Vallandry hotels are **ski-in ski-out**. Technically you could ski into and more-or-less out of those in Arc 2000, but you won't find anything like the convenience level you get in Courchevel or Tignes. But all the resorts are so small and everywhere is so close to one lift or another that it doesn't really matter where you stay.

Some hotels will only accept week-long **reservations**, especially if you are booking a long time in advance. Every front-of-house employee will speak **english**, so unless you have a quibble with a cleaning lady you will be able to survive with no French at all. But hotels are where you will notice a difference if you can speak in French. Staff are more likely to be more sympathetic to questions (or complaints) if you make the effort to communicate with them in their language.

Unless otherwise stated, all have bedrooms with en-suite (a shower or a bath). All the resorts have ample **parking** within a short distance of the hotels.

la cachette***

☎ 0479 077050
📞 0479 077401
@ hotel.cachette@wanadoo.fr
𝒲³ -
🛏 72 (½)

p85 d2

27

Entirely central and hence very convenient, La Cachette in 1600 is also a very pleasant and friendly feeling hotel. There's a gym for those who don't ski hard enough, and if you manage to get your dog over the border they'll be happy to let you hide him in your room. Also equipped with a restaurant, a bar, TVs in the rooms and so on - La Cachette is nothing to get too excited about but it is far and away the most comfortable place to spend your evenings in 1600.

explorers'**

☎ 0479 041600
📞 0479 072141
@ arc1600@hotelexplorers.com
𝒲³ hotelexplorers.com
🛏 32 (b&b, ½)

p85 f1

At the southern extent of 1600, the Explorers' has the ignominious distinction of being part of the ugly first sight of the resort that every visitor to Les Arcs sees on the road up the hill. Fortunately once you're there you don't have to look at the outside much. The Explorers' is 2* comfort at 2* prices - not fancy, but not disastrous for your wallet either.

accommodation

hotel du golf***

☎ 0479 414343
✆ 0479 073428
@ hotel.du.golf@meava.fr
w^3 -
🛏 64 (b&b, ½)

28

Slap bang in the middle of 1800's shops and bars, the Hôtel du Golf is as close to luxury as you can get in Les Arcs (though it still falls very much in the mid-range bracket in terms of facilities and prices). The rooms are spacious, the restaurant serves truly gourmet food and the bar is the only place in the resort where you won't feel silly wearing a jacket (and you might feel silly if you're not). There are downsides - it's not even vaguely plush, some things that ought to work - like the internet points - don't, but it isn't overly expensive and until Arc 1950's hotel opens you can't do a great deal better.

club du soleil***

☎ 0479 040909
✆ 0479 040999
@ -
w^3 villagesclubdusoleil.com
🛏 72 (b&b, ½)

On a par with the Hôtel du Golf in terms of quality of rooms and service, the Club du Soleil (also in 1800) offers an all inclusive package of ski and boot rental along with your room and has a variety of child-specific packages available so you can ditch the young'uns and head off up the slopes in peace. It's out in Charmettoger, which is a short walk from the main action - but if you're coming with the family that's possibly not such a bad thing.

and the rest

In the small and rather pointless Village des Deux Têtes, just above 1600, is the very normal hotel **beguin** (2*, t 0479 070292, i hotelbeguin.com). If you want to stay in 1800 but can't get a room in the Golf or the Soleil, try the **mercure** (3*, t 0479 076500, i mercure.com) or the **charmettoger** (3*, t 0479 074979). Arc 2000 is home to the **aiguille rouge** (2*, t 0479 075707, i vvf-vacances.fr) and the **mélèzes** (3*, t 0479 075050). There are also hotels in Peisey-Vallandry - the **emeraude** (2*, t 0479 079446) just above the centre of Vallandry, or for a view of the new Paradiski link try **la vanoise** (2*, t 0479 079219).

chalets

Chalet holidays cater for those who want to stay in a more relaxed setting, but don't want to fend for themselves. Because of the relatively small amount of chalet accommodation in Les Arcs, if you want a certain thing you may have to stay in a certain place, and vice versa.

tour operators

There are plenty of English tour operators in Les Arcs and Peisey-Vallandry, and many offer chalet accommodation of one sort or another. True chalet accommodation - where you stay in what is effectively a house, with a kitchen and some bedrooms and a single host who cooks your meals for you - can only really be found in Peisey-Vallandry. Elsewhere, the 'chalet-style' accommodation works in roughly the same way, but your room(s) are part of a larger building that looks like a chalet only about 5 times the size. Either way, you will be looked after by a chalet host or tour operator rep, and provided with breakfast, afternoon tea and on 6 nights out of 7 an evening meal with wine. Most tour operators also organise flights and transfers, and as a general rule you can expect the service you receive to be approximately equivalent to the price you pay. Unless you book the whole place you take pot luck with your fellow guests - it can be a war-zone or the beginning of a beautiful friendship - but at least you know you all like snow.

1800 has a small cluster of chalet accommodation (a short drive further up the hill) in a new development, which also has its own rental shop and a couple of restaurants. It's quiet and secluded, but it is far enough away from the resort that you may not fancy walking back up the hill at 2am if you've made your way down for a quiet shandy. In 2000 the chalets are further down the hill than the resort itself, and also have their own little community, with 2 bars, a supermarket and a rental shop. The majority of the accommodation is run by English highstreet tour operators and as a result the community is almost exclusively English. Further down the hill Peisey-Vallandry is a more authentic mountain community and the chalet accommodation gives you a broader range of choices, including some small privately run chalets along with those controlled by tour operators.

accommodation

independents

Information on privately run chalets is not as easy to find. Almost all are in the Peisey-Vallandry area, and your best bets are Plan-Peisey Accommodation, the tourist office, or good old Google.

apartments

30

What Les Arcs does have is a lot of apartments. Self-catering accommodation is everywhere - perhaps largely because of the resort's popularity with families and schools. Mucking-in and cooking for yourself is doubtless the cheapest way to ski, though with the construction of Arc 1950 you can now also cook for yourself in style. Wherever you stay you can expect to be provided with kitchen facilities and utensils, along with bed linen and a simple kitchen kit. In the most basic apartments this means a fridge, a hob, pots and pans, a few knives and forks and some washing-up liquid. Luxuries like TV connection are extra. In the more upmarket options you may get a microwave and a widescreen TV, and pleasant little touches like coffee and hot chocolate in the cupboard.

The accommodation agencies renting out self-catering apartments are numerous and count among them the usual suspects of Maeva (i maeva.fr) and CIS Immobilier (i cis-immobiliercom) - a full list can be obtained from any of the tourist offices.

youth hostel

Of sorts. If price is the biggest factor in where you stay, it may be worth your while thinking about staying in Les Arcs UCPA (t 0327 475661, i upca.com) - as long as you are aged 18-39 years. A French run entity (translating as 'a union of youth associations') they offer a variety of ski packages on a weekly basis and for some weekends - bed and board, ski hire, lift pass and ski instruction are all included in the price. Accommodation is in shared rooms and a full entertainment package is organised in true modern day Butlins style - with a French twist.

camping

For those on a real budget, there is a site for camper vans in 1600 (t 0479 071451) equipped with water and electricity points.

bourg st. maurice

If you don't mind commuting in to the ski area every day, staying in Bourg St. Maurice is a way to find a broader range of accommodation, with a bit more individuality and at a reasonable price and with the benefits of being in a town rather than a tiny resort. Your trip to the skiing takes 7 minutes on the Les Arcs funicular up to 1600 - the train runs 7:30am-7:20pm, meaning you can catch the first lift, ski a full day and enjoy a lazy après vin chaud before you head down in the evening. Occasionally - and inappropriately - referred to as Bourg St. Moritz, the valley floor town of Bourg is not at first glance obviously a part of Les Arcs. But it is marketed under the same banner, and the funicular link to Arc 1600 makes staying in a town and skiing in Les Arcs a viable choice for those who want to avoid the claustrophobia of the high altitude resorts. It is too large to be given adequate coverage here, but in brief it provides acceptable skiing access alongside town-sized diversity. While some of Les Arcs' resorts may be a little lacking on choice. It's not really the place from which to experience the full extent of Paradiski, but for self-drive skiers who like variety it makes a perfect base from which to explore the various resorts of the Haute Savoie. **hotels** range the 0* Le Savoyard (t 0479 075351, i le-savoyard.com) to the more luxurious 3* Autantic (t 0479 010170, i hotel-autantic.com). For more information on all hotels in Bourg contact the tourist office (t 0479 070493, i bourgsaintmaurice.com). Alternatively you can opt for the **chalet** experience. Vanilla Ski (t 01932 860696, i vanillaski.com), an English-run company have a chalet 2 miles outside of Bourg - an ideal base for exploring the skiing in Les Arcs, or further afield in La Plagne or the Espace Killy ski area.

31

Once you have arrived in Les Arcs and found where you are staying, there are a few things to do before you can get on to the snow. For many people, long queues and language barriers make this the worst part of the holiday. Starting with lift passes, the following pages take you step by step through the process and how to survive it.

32

The lift system in Les Arcs is currently more state-of-transition than state-of-the-art. The advent of Paradiski means no more will you have to flash your ID to the nice girl as you get onto every lift. It will take a while to phase in, but from 2004 the system officially goes hands free. You buy a card with a computer chip in it that activates the turnstile as you approach it. At the moment only a few lifts will run the system, but over the next few seasons the entire Paradiski area will be upgraded. Aside from the obvious hassle reduction, a totally electronic system means you don't need a photo, ever, at all, for any number of days. In addition there are many potential advantages to this system.

the future

Eventually the computerised system will allow you to be much more specific about when you are actually going to ski. It is kind of the ski-resort version of tailor-made package holidays: you could, for instance, buy a pass for 5 days (instead of the usual 6) and just take a day off midweek without wasting

a day of your pass. You could buy a pass for just afternoons. And so on. The potential is huge. Once you've bought the pass (for €3 or so) you can keep it, and re-use it every time you come back. Clearly this is all good for encouraging return visits, but it also has the enormous benefit of allowing you to charge your card over the internet, so you won't have to stand around in a queue in resort. But this stuff doesn't exist yet - and though the future is bright, the future is also expensive.

les arcs or paradiski?

If you feel the need to expand your horizons across the valley, your options for accessing the Paradiski area are many. With a standard pass for Les Arcs you can buy a 1 day Paradiski extension. The next option up is the Paradiski *Découverte* pass, which gives you 1 day in La Plagne for very slightly less than buying the extension. The attraction of the Découverte pass is that it also qualifies you for 1 day's skiing in the 3

Vallées, the Espace Killy, Pralognan or Les Saisies. This is also true of the standard Paradiski pass, which gives you full access to all of Paradiski on every day the pass is valid. The Paradiski pass is significantly more expensive than the Les Arcs pass, but cheaper than buying 2 La Plagne day-trips. If this all seems a little complicated, it gets worse when you factor in the other possible reductions for families and specific lifts - but if you take a bit of time to work out what you want to do you may save yourself a few Euros.

handy to know

The introduction of Paradiski has created a complicated ménage à trois: the uniting of Les Arcs and La Plagne means that there are now 3 lift companies looking after what is officially 1 area (Paradiski itself is a separate entity). This makes for a lot of diplomatic to-ing and fro-ing which fortunately you never need to think about. You can buy any kind of pass from the lift pass offices in all the resorts. Arc 1800 has 2, one at either end of the commercial centre, and the other resorts have one each. All of them close during the lunchtime siesta during the week, but all are open all day on Saturdays.

If you are **over 72** or **under 6** years old, you ski for free, though you still need to get a pass that shows this. Passes are cheaper very **early** and very **late** in the season - largely because not all the area will be open during these periods. And now it gets a little complicated. **families** of 4 or more get a simple reduction on their passes (for just Les Arcs or the whole of Paradiski), but also have the option of buying transferable passes so that dad can ski with the kids on 1 day while mum goes shopping, and then mum can use the same pass the next day while dad stays in bed all day. Or whatever. You can buy a pass specifically for the area around 1600 and 1800, or for the area around 1950 and 2000, or for the area around Villaroger. You can buy a **snowpark** pass that only works for the Cachette, Vagère, Arpette and Clair Blanc lifts. And there are other **options**, aimed at **ski-tourers** and **pedestrians**. If you're confused ask your rep or at the tourist office.

33

Another advantage of the new hands-free system is that because everything gets recorded on a computer, you get lift pass **insurance**. You will be given a number when you buy your pass, which is a bit like a PIN number for a bank card. Quote that number when you lose it and they will void the old pass and give you a new one. **carré neige** is not included as standard with lift passes, but it is available for a small daily supplement - you will be asked whether or not you want it when you buy your pass. If you have not organised your own already, the insurance is highly recommended. It covers you for all on-piste incidents, including blood wagon and helicopter recovery.

With a few exceptions, much of the rental market in Les Arcs is controlled by the major chain stores. Names like Twinner, Sport 2000 and Ski Set appear in every resort (apart from 1950) - and with these places you know what you are getting. It's a bit like buying your books from Waterstones or Ottakars - the range is pretty good and the service is pretty good. What these stores lack is the attention and focus of an independently run business. Employees tend to be seasonnaires - which doesn't mean the service is bad, but does mean that the chap setting your skis up probably only has a year or maybe 2 years' experience. And because they're run by a central body, if you have a specific desire for something a little obscure, you're unlikely to find it - to continue the analogy, you might have to go to a specialist bookshop. This is particularly true for snowboarders, as the range of rental boards in ski-specific shops is limited and generally very uninspiring.

34

handy to know

Getting the **right equipment** will ensure you fully enjoy your holiday. Your feet will hurt if you don't get boots that fit well so don't be embarrassed to persevere until you find a pair that fits. If your boots cause you problems after you have tested them out, take them back - all the shops will help you find a more suitable pair. Unless you know you want a specific type or make of ski, take the advice of the ski fitter. They

are the experts and will know which is the best ski for you based on your ability and age. All of the stores employ either competent or native **English** speakers, and all the staff know enough English to fit you with the right skis and boots... as with most places trying a little French won't hurt, but unless you are a confident speaker this is one area where it's probably best to operate in a language you are comfortable with.

The chain stores generally stock a broad range of Salomon and Rossignol skis, sometimes along with a small selection of less prominent brands like Atomic and Head. As a normal skier this is pretty much all you will need - but for telemarking or touring skis you will have to hunt around.

At most shops you can take out **insurance** (except on test skis) to cover accidental breakage, loss or theft. Unfortunately skis do get stolen or taken by accident - with so many people skiing on similar skis it's easy to confuse yours with those belonging to somebody else. When you stop for lunch or après, it's a good idea to swap one of your skis with a friend so you both have a mis-matched pair. This helps ensure that nobody will pick up your skis, either by mistake or otherwise.

There's not a great deal of inspiration in the rental market - but a few stores are the goats among the sheep.

for skis

The first of 2 **ogier** stores has opened in Arc 1950 - the second will be completed in time for 2005-2006 winter season. It is an expansive store that stocks quality equipment - more so for skiers than boarders, who are catered for across the road - and very much in the same vein as the Ogier stores in Val d'Isère and Chamonix. There is also a range of somewhat less functional clothing for those more attuned to winter fashion than winter sports.

A quality rental shop that also makes for good browsing is **christine sports** in 1600. Service is friendly and there is a separate board-specific section. They know what they're talking about and are happy to talk about it.

for boards

concept snowboards in 1950 is a top-end snowboard shop that stocks many of the better known brands. Rental boards are mostly Burtons, but if you're looking to buy you will have a pretty full choice. It's also a good store for clothes shopping and general browsing, and as with everywhere else in 1950, the staff are flawlessly helpful.

A small but excellent shop by the snow front in Les Villards, **le petit passage** in 1800 is the best board option for rentals, servicing, accessories (not including baggy trousers) and general attention to detail. They are also very friendly people with a love for the sport and the resort, and will be happy to chat away about the weather or whatever pops into your mind.

for other equipment

For more specialist equipment, such as touring skins and avalanche packs, the bigger chain stores should be able to kit you out. Rental shops also stock a wide range of ski clothing - although brands differ from shop to shop so you will need to shop around if you are looking for a specific make - as well as all the accessories you can think of. There is little difference from what you would pay for the same clothes in the UK.

35

lessons & guiding

ski schools

As with many French resorts, the biggest presence in Les Arcs is exerted by the ESF (Ecole de Ski Français). Their trademarks are red jackets and enough instructors that if they stood on each other's shoulders they would stretch to the moon and back. Service is generally good, and simply thanks to the law of averages it works out that some of them are fantastic instructors and some aren't particularly good at all. They generally allocate the instructors pretty sensibly - if you book a private lesson for your kids they will try to choose someone that's good with kids - but the demand during peak season is such that you basically get what you get, in a sort of lucky dip fashion. Smaller ski schools tend to be more specialised and you can be more sure about who will be teaching you - and some only offer private instruction.

specifics

group lessons are the cheapest way to learn to ski. When you book you will be asked your level of skiing/boarding ability, either by the colour of piste you are comfortable on, the number of weeks you have skied before, or by the vague 'beginner/intermediate/advanced' pigeonholes. In practice the divisions aren't as accurate as they could be - some people overestimate their ability or misunderstand words like 'confident' and 'controlled', so to and extent the level of your group is pot luck. If you

are honest about your skill level you are likely to find yourself (vaguely) in the right place. If you have the money, **private lessons** are without question the way forward. Once you're past the basics, individual attention is the best way to significantly improve your technique and is often better value. If you can get a group of 4 or more the individual price per day is similar to the average price per day for group lessons, with the advantage that you go where you want to go and practise what you want to practise. The length of private lessons varies from school to school, but generally the divisions are simply for a half day (morning or afternoon) or a full day. A half day will be 3 hours of instruction on one side of lunch. **prices** are pretty standard across the board - though you may pay a little more for the smaller companies, there's not much in it. If you book group lessons you can have a week's worth of half-day instruction for only a little more than it costs to rent your skis. Private lessons (and guides) are a different story, but again you won't find too much variation in what the different schools charge. Either make your **booking** before you get to Les Arcs - by email, fax or phone - or once you're in resort, in person at the ski school office. Always pre-book in peak season, as there are not enough instructors to meet demand - schools recommend booking at least 2 weeks (and longer in peak weeks) in advance. To confirm your booking, the schools will need your name, level of ability and a credit card number. Each of the Les Arcs resorts are so small that **meeting points** are pretty obvious. No matter where you're staying you won't have to go far - the snow front of each resort functions as the main rendezvous (above Les Villards for 1800), unless you arrange something different when you book. It is illegal to teach in France without a qualification recognised by the French establishment. In effect this means that the majority of **instructors** in France are French, as few with 'international' qualifications are accepted and the equivalence race test that foreign instructors must pass is extremely difficult. But this approach gives you the advantage of knowing that your instructor is at the least a very competent skier or boarder. Almost all instructors speak good **English** and there are also instructors who speak every other language - though you will need to book a long way in advance should you want instruction in a language less common to the Alps. Lessons take place **whatever the weather**, unless the entire lift system is closed in which case the school will refund the full lesson price. They will also refund you if you are ill or have an accident and can produce a valid medical certificate. If you cancel a lesson for any other reason, your chances of getting a refund are relative to how much notice you give the school, and how charming you are when you cancel.

esf

G

📞 by resort
📱 by resort
@ by resort
www³ esflesarcs.com
✉ les villards (1800)

37

The ESF is the oldest ski school in the Alps, and becoming an instructor is a difficult enough process that you are guaranteed a quality skier as your teacher. What you are not guaranteed is that you will be taught the latest techniques - older instructors who themselves learned on older skis may not be entirely up to speed on carving. It has been said that there are as many ways to ski as there are ESF instructors. On the other side of the coin, many of the younger instructors teach both skiing and snowboarding, and there are charismatic and competent teachers in abundance. Except 1950 all of Les Arcs' resorts have an ESF office: 1600 t 0479 074309, 1800 t 0479 074031, 2000 t 0479 074752 and Vallandry t 0479 079584. 1800 has the largest number of instructors (though it makes sense to go to the school in your resort) and is the only one equipped for disabled skiing. All branches offer the standard group and private lessons for adults and children throughout the entire season.

arc aventures

☎ 0479 074128
📞 0479 077327
@ arc.aventures@wanadoo.fr
ᴡᵂ³ arc-aventures.com
📧 front de neige, les villards (1800)

38 A sizeable company that - as is evident from the name - only operates in Les Arcs (based in 1800). Group lessons take place in the morning, (9:30am-midday). Private lessons are available in 1 or 2 hour chunks along with the half- and full-day options, and their guides offer all the usual off-piste options, including cross-country skiing, ski touring, heliskiing and non-skiing pursuits like snowshoeing, snowmobiling and ice climbing. Their snowboard programme runs much as their ski programme, and children of 4-13 years are catered for in specialist lessons. They're an enthusiastic bunch, and if you don't like red jackets, these chaps tend to wear green ones.

spirit 1950

☎ 0479 042572
📞 by 0479 042572
@ contact@spirit1950.com
ᴡᵂ³ spirit1950.com
📧 arc 1950

Spirit is as new as the resort (1950) they're based in - but of course their instructors are very experienced and their approach to lessons draws on the friendly and entertaining ethos so prevalent in everything Arc 1950. Group lessons are limited to a maximum of 10 people and they run a snowboard course that includes equipment rental from Concept (➡ skis, boots & boards) (everything in 1950 is tied together). All the other options are available too, in addition to which - and as they're proud of reminding you - they look cool, because they wear black.

guides

To get the best from Les Arcs' outstanding unpisted area, you will need to hire a guide. From the lifts you don't see what's on the other side of the various ridges - and if you find yourself watching people wandering off up some face or other and wondering about where everyone's going, the way to find out is to hire a guide. There is hidden off-piste to suit every ability level - but you should not explore it without the services of a professional.

The difference between **guides and instructors** is fundamental - instructing is about 'how' and guiding is about 'where'. Ski instructors are not permitted to take you off-piste and you should not ask them to. In contrast the limiting factor with a guide is your own ability. If you are competent enough they will take you anywhere you want to go. There is no question of a guide's **ability**. Becoming one takes years and requires an intimate knowledge of everything the mountains have to offer particularly how to be safe in this notoriously unpredictable environment. Guides are not just expert skiers, first and foremost they are mountaineers: physically fit individuals, with extensive experience of mountain rescue, practice and procedure. They are also proficient rock and ice climbers and are competent and comfortable in all types of conditions. During the course of qualifying, they are tested on alpine technique, avalanche rescue and first aid, to name but a few. The very definition of a safe pair of hands.

And how do you find these illustrious mountain men? Most of the ski schools have a number of guides on their books. The Bureau des Guides (to which all guides belong) is based in 1800 (t 0479 077119). A professional outfit of people who spend almost all of their time out of sight of the pistes. Many of the guides are qualified in a variety of disciplines, and just as they offer the full gamut of off-piste experience the Bureau also offers activities like parapenting and snowmobiling. If you have a specific request or want them to come up with an interesting idea, just ask.

A couple of the ski schools also have more of a leaning to life away from the markers. **initial-snow** (t 0612 457291, i initial-snow.com) is a small and specialised company of instructors and guides based in Bourg St. Maurice - but with an outlet in Christina Sports in Arc 1600 - who are happiest in the backcountry. Also in Bourg is **darentasia** (t 0479 041681, i darentasia.com) a small outfit which is actually a parapenting school who also run a number of specialist off-piste courses in groups of no more than 6 people for a full single day or over 5 mornings. Though both companies are based in Bourg St. Maurice they will meet you where you are.

39

The **price** of hiring a guide isn't cheap. For a private guide the bigger your group, the less you pay individually. A day's guiding for up to 5 people costs around CHF500 - but you are better off spending the money and coming back alive. You need to have mountain rescue insurance to go with one of them. Guides are obliged to provide you with an avalanche transceiver and all other relevant equipment.

If you decide to hire a guide, don't underestimate how **fit** you need to be to get the most out of the experience. Whilst the guide will cater the day to the standard of the least able skier in the group, he may still lead you along some tiring traverses or climbs to reach the best snow.

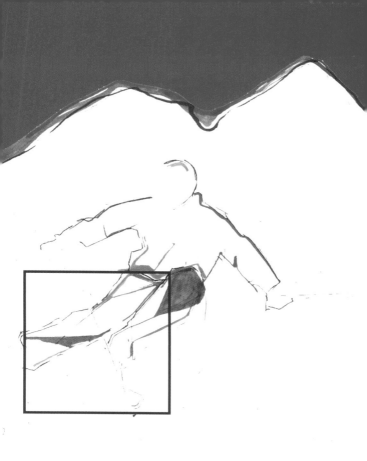

the skiing

The skiing is some of the best that the Alps can offer. Between the markers there is everything you could possibly want - a network of blue cruises, plenty of high speed reds, and an array of black bump runs that will shake up your senses. But the real joy of skiing in Les Arcs is the off-piste - the available terrain is varied, vast, and largely unskied by the majority of the tourist population. Some of the best runs in the resort can still have fresh snow a week after a fall - and even if you only ski what you can see from a lift you have plenty of options, including some outstanding tree skiing in Peisey-Vallandry. The skiing in the other half of the huge Paradiski area has a very different character to that around Les Arcs. In general, La Plagne's pistes are gentler, the sectors are more varied, and the terrain rolls more. Objectively it is not as good an area as Les Arcs - but it is a change of scene.

pistes

In most resorts, there are times when you will find yourself stopping halfway down some piste or other, wondering who was responsible for calling it a red when it clearly ought to be a black - or a blue. This experience, however, is very unlikely to happen in Les Arcs. The pistes are well-rated, and for the most part well signposted and well-groomed. Lower down and especially close to Arc 1800, the terrain can become rutty and bumpy, and there is rarely the cushy

---

snapshot

vital statistics
les arcs
200kms of pistes - 1 green, 53 blues, 31 reds & 19 blacks
lifts - 1 funicular, 4 cable cars, 3 gondolas, 31 chairlifts & 16 draglifts
highest point - 3227m

paradiski
420kms of pistes - 12 greens, 125 blues, 64 reds & 31 blacks
144 lifts - 1 funicular, 6 cable cars, 10 gondolas, 65 chairlifts & 61 draglifts
highest point - 3250m

---

corduroy feel that Courchevel skiers will be used to, but on the whole the piste system is both well organised and well maintained. The piste system follows the same colour-coding used in all ski areas throughout Europe (➥ 'pistes' in the glossary). You should only use the piste colour-coding as a general guide - as personal feelings can vary.

off-piste

Whether your taste is for nipping off the side of the piste or hiking to the other end of a ridge, Les Arcs has plenty of entertainment in store. Vallandry's trees are perfect for bad weather, and when the snowfall stops and the clouds break the opportunities are many. The 2 main peaks, the Grive and Rouge, host between them any number of possible lines - some of them well known and some of them less so. Add in La Plagne and the Bellecôte glacier, and you're in powder heaven. Unlike in the Swiss resorts no itinerary routes are marked on the official map.

lifts

Paradiski and Arc 1950 have between them procured a hefty amount of cash for the Les Arcs lift system. This will eventually bring Les Arcs in line with the slick and efficient systems in the neighbouring 3 Vallées and Espace Killy, with new lifts popping up all over the mountain. 2004 sees a new lift from Vallandry, and the following season the poor snowpark access will be addressed with a 6-man chair replacing the Arpette and a long-overdue park specific draglift replacing the Clair Blanc. Most of the lifts open in early December, the remainder are operational by Christmas. The lower part of the Villaroger sector runs out of snow first - Peisey-Vallandry also suffers from low altitude snow-sickness but the need to keep the Paradiski link open means that there is good artificial snow cover. Up around 1950 and 2000 the snow lasts longer - usually until the end of April. During shorter daylight hours in the depths of winter, the lifts close earlier in the day than later on in the season. Opening and closing times are noted at the bottom of some lifts, or alternatively the tourist office has full details of approximate times for the whole season.

the areas

For the purposes of this guide the

Paradiski ski area has been divided into 12 sectors which are arranged in sequence from top to bottom (east to west) on the overview map (➜ inside back cover flap) - starting with Villaroger in Les Arcs and ending with Montalbert in La Plagne. There are 5 sectors describing the skiing above the resorts of Les Arcs (a-e) and 7 for the skiing above the resorts of La Plagne (f-l). In this chapter you'll find a description of how to get to and from the slopes, the general characteristics and aspect of the area, and detail of the pistes, the off-piste, the mountain restaurants and the local après for each area. In this chapter the ski areas for Les Arcs are described first, as follows:

43

les arcs areas

villaroger (map a)
aiguille rouge (map b)
arc 1600 (map c)
arc 1800 (map d)
vallandry (map e)

The areas above La Plagne's resorts follow in the order that you would pass through them after taking the Vanoise Express:

la plagne areas

montchavin (map f)
roche de mio (map g)
bellecôte glacier (map h)
champagny (map i)
plagne centre (map j)
aime la plagne & 1800 (map k)
montalbert (map l)

At the back of the book there is a more detailed table of lift information and a ski map for each area (the piste colours correspond to those used by the resort).

coming & going

Getting going depends very much on where you are staying. The 3 main lifts from **arc 1800** are the Vagère chairlift for the northern side or for Arc 1600, the Villards chairlift for the south side or for Peisey-Vallandry, and the Transarc gondola for Arc 2000 and the Aiguille Rouge. The Charmettoger chairlift is incredibly slow, and doesn't go anywhere you couldn't get to more quickly by another route. Coming home is pretty simple - the Bois de l'Ours or Plagnettes chairlifts from Arc 2000, the Cachette or Gollet from Arc 1600, and the Vallandry chairlift from Vallandry, all of which allow you to cruise down to the 1800 resort.

From **arc 1600** the 2 main lifts are the Mont Blanc and Cachette chairlifts - the Cachette also allows you to make your way into the 1800 sector, as does the Gollet chairlift. Coming back to 1600 you need the Bois de l'Ours or Comborcières chairlifts from the Arc 2000 sector. Getting home from 1800 you can take either the Vagère or Carreley chairlifts, and from Vallandry you want the Vallandry chairlift and then the Vagère or Carreley from Arc 1800.

arc 1950 and **arc 2000** are right in the thick of the skiing already - you can ski down to the Varet gondola from 2000 and the Marmottes and Bois de

l'Ours lifts are right below 1950 - the Bois de l'Ours being the best route to the other side of the ridge for 1800, 1600 and Peisey-Vallandry. The Lanchettes chairlift from Arc 2000 leads over to the Villaroger sector.

The main lift from **vallandry** carries the same name as the town, and from winter 2004 it is joined by the Grizzli which will also provide access to the main ski area. From Plan-Peisey head up into the skiing on the Peisey chairlift, or across to La Plagne on the Vanoise Express. Coming home from the rest of Les Arcs is easy - you can ski straight down to Vallandry from the top of the Villards, Transarc or Charmettoger lifts, or if you can find it you can cruise home on the Fôret piste which turns towards Vallandry above the far end of Charmettoger.

For any of the skiing in La Plagne, head to Plan-Peisey and the Vanoise Express in the Peisey-Vallandry sector.

beginners

The slopes above Vallandry have 2 beginner-specific areas, and all of 1600, 1800 and 2000 have areas that are intended just for those making their first few stuttering turns. Unusually for France, there are no green pistes, but despite this Les Arcs is a good place to learn no matter what your age or how daring you are - 1800 has children's areas in the resort, and the ski schools are well versed in coping with learners.

For those who are starting to step out on their own, the best choice is probably the run down to 1800 from the mid-station of the Transarc, and the gentle area just above Arc 2000 and 1950.

intermediates

If your niche is the red run, you will not be stuck for somewhere to go. Arc 1800 boasts the richest blend, and is the best place for those crossing the blue-red boundary. Peisey-Vallandry has a lot to offer too, and though there is less choice above 2000 the quality is no lower - space for carving practice, a park to get your first brief airtime, moguls aplenty and by-the-piste off-piste. You won't be bored.

experts

Though you may not be turned on by the limited gradient of Les Arcs network of blues and reds, the length and breadth of the unpisted black runs down from the Aiguille Rouge will be more than enough to get your heart pumping. Peisey-Vallandry is a tree-skiers dream. If you like short hikes before your off-piste descents there are some routes that you will want to do again and again. And the Vanoise Express means you can now ski the infamous Bellecôte glacier without having to worry about how to get over to La Plagne.

boarders

The areas is as good for those on one plank as it is for those on two. The medium gradient of much of the pisted skiing makes it an ideal place to learn, and there are only a few draglifts and none of those are long. The park has enough top level challenge to amuse anyone who likes to get airborne, and away from the pistes there are plenty of options for freeriders - though many of the off-piste runs that head towards Villaroger have a very flat exit which may leave you cursing and walking.

snowpark

There is only 1 park in Les Arcs, on the slopes above 1800. It has plenty of challenges and it's pretty good no matter what your ability - and if you're looking for the right spot to show off your new baggy boarding pants, it is also the designated lunch spot for much of the snowboarding seasonnaire community. For more variety you can head over to La Plagne where there are 3 parks and a half-pipe.

non-skiers

Though not the best destination for non-skiers, there are 30kms of walking pistes around Les Arcs. These are mostly very pleasant forest hikes - the route between 1800 and Vallandry is a gentle stroll through the trees which sees a lot of pedestrian traffic. For spectacular views, you can take the Transarc from 1800 up to the Ice Grotto, in the shadow of the Aiguille Grive, and those in 1950 or 2000 can take the Varet gondola and then the Aiguille Rouge cable car to the top of the peak of the same name at 3227m.

45

Something of an aside to the main ski domain, the pistes leading down towards Villaroger at the eastern end of the area are overlooked by the majority of Les Arcs holidaymakers, and as such make an excellent destination to escape the crowds. It is best skied in the morning, as it catches sunshine before anywhere else in Les Arcs - but by the same token it is cold in the afternoon once the sun has gone, and once you've used the limited pisted area to warm up your legs you will probably be best satisfied elsewhere.

46

access
The only on-piste ways into the Villaroger sector are the Lanchettes chairlift from Arc 2000 or the long ski down from the top of the Aiguille Rouge cable car.

pistes
The first sniff of something gentle is the **blue** track that leads round to Comborcières - very flat, and very definitely a track. Lower down towards Villaroger there are more blues, of a more sensible width, but there is little variety or entertainment.

The **reds** are sustained and unthreatening - enough to make intermediates work hard but not enough to scare them. When conditions are poor in early or late season they can be a struggle - either patchy or icy, or both.

map a

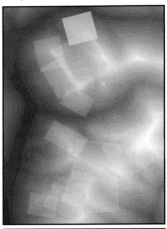

snapshot

out of interest
highest point - 2400m
aspect - ne
pistes - some blues, a couple of reds
& a grotty black
off-piste - limited, trees
restaurants - 2 worth a visit in Le Pré
and 1 on the mountain

highlights & hotspots
morning sunshine
cold in the afternoon (particularly on
the plan des violettes chair)
not many people
snow gets thin in late season

The 1 **black** run isn't much steeper than the reds - its classification is due as much to it being tricky in poor conditions, and possibly also to a more haphazard or less regular approach to grooming.

off-piste

There's not much skiing away from the pistes - the trees are a little too close together and so are a little inaccessible. Villaroger is, however, the finishing point for some of Les Arcs' less well publicised off-piste runs... you need to bribe a local to find out about them.

eating & drinking

There are 2 food choices where the pistes run out in Le Pré - a large and standard offering (La Ferme) and a tiny and out-of-the-way one (L'Aiguille Rouge). **la ferme** does good omelettes and in spite of being pretty normal and generally busy it still has the village friendliness of somewhere that isn't too affected by mass ski-tourism. Take that village atmosphere and square it and you've got **l'aiguille rouge**. Alternatively you can try the **belliou la fumée** (t 0479 072913) and **au pré gourmand** (t 0479 073746), which are around the corner underneath Arc 1950, but which you can get to directly on the long (and flat) track that starts just under the top of the Plan des Violettes chairlift (➥ aiguille rouge).

On the mountain, standard self-service food and a cramped entrance at **le solliet** belie what is a very pleasant and quite amusing little restaurant. The inside is lovely and cosy, and a welcome and homely change from so many varnished wooden food halls. There is an open fire and authentic decoration, and though the upstairs is disappointingly modern the ground floor seating is lovely in a higgledy-piggledy sort of way. And if you are a collector of random hand-painted wooden stuff you can get that here too.

47

By lunchtime the sun will have more-or-less gone from the Villaroger side of the skiing - for **a picnic** lunch on the mountain you are better off somewhere else.

getting home

There are 2 routes out of the Villaroger sector. The most obvious is the Plan des Violettes chair followed by the Droset chair and a quick ski back to Arc 2000. Alternatively you can take the winding track round the mountain down to the Comborcières and Pré St Esprit charlifts (and the Au Pré Gourmand and Belliou la Fumée restaurants).

The Aiguille Rouge, the area above Arc 2000 and 1950, is very much an area of 2 halves. If you approach it from 1800 the runs are gentle and cruisy, but on the eastern side up towards the Aiguille Rouge everything is red or black. Camera bashers can head for the Ice Grotto, fine diners for Les Chalets de L'Arc, and those with more action-based personalities can hone their mogul skills and put in some high speed turns. If you know where you're going, this is also the launching point for some wonderful off-piste routes, and if you're completely mad, this is where you can try out speed skiing.

48

access
From the 1800 side of the ridge, the main route into the Aiguille Rouge sector is via the Transarc gondola - but you can also get over on any number of chairlifts.

pistes
It's hard to work up a sweat on the **blues** - they are level enough that you won't get a head of steam going anywhere. They are best used as ways to get somewhere else - or for families with small children, the windy runs from the Ice Grotto to the Marmottes chair tend to be less busy than most places.

If your mogul technique isn't up to the length and breadth of the black runs, head to the top of the Plagnettes chairlift (or Bosses drag) for a brief practice run on a **red** instead. The best

map b

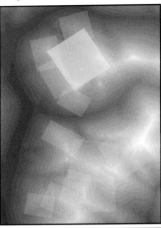

snapshot

out of interest
highest point - 3227m
aspect - e, s, w
pistes - gentle blues, a variety of red & lots and lots of blacks
off-piste - extensive
restaurants - 6

highlights & hotspots
the highest bakery in europe - les chalets de l'arc restaurant
lots of people
lots of queues
lots of bumps
lots of off-piste

of the pisted reds is from the top of the Grand Col chairlift - don't bother with the Aiguille Rouge cable car unless you want to ski black, as the reds from there are little more than tracks.

The **blacks** are all long and exhausting mogul runs. You can take your pick - those accessed by the Aiguille Rouge cable car are less skied by virtue of being more difficult to get to. The lines under the Varet gondola are a little less steep but provide ample challenge for all but the best skiers - the same is true of the lines from the Comborcières and Bois de l'Ours chairs on the other side of the area. For a steep run away from the bumps you can try your hand (or leg) on the Kilometre Lancé.

off-piste

If you're up early on a powder day you will find excellent skiing pretty much wherever you go. The less obvious lines are down to the Comborcières chair

below 1950, from either ridgeline. There's also plenty to be found from the Aiguille Rouge cable car, if you know where to go. The Plagnettes chair leads to the ridge from where you can access the Aiguille Grive off-piste descent (➡ off-piste & touring).

eating & drinking

les chalets de l'arc (t 0479 041540) is the highest bakery in Europe, and rightly proud of it. It is difficult to think of how a mountain restaurant could be better, unless you want refuge hut authenticity. There's none of that, but in its place is a large restaurant serving utterly delicious food from huge indoor and outdoor sections that manage - through the use of different levels - to feel intimate no matter where you sit. The outside is much like the inside except without the roof (properly laid tables, attentive waiter service, trays and trolleys of fruit and desserts), the food is superb, and the bread is better than you will find in any of the resorts themselves. Fresh baked every day on site, it ranges from simple pastries and croissants to the unparalleled *chasson de boulanger* - effectively stuffed bread that might just as well have been made by AW-T on a Saturday morning TV show. And in a lesson to the restaurants of the Espace Killy, in spite of all this you still don't have to pay for the toilets.

Though in a prime location, next to the Ice Grotto and in the shadow of the

49

Aiguille Grive, **la crèche** is a very standard restaurant. The name is appropriate - it may as well be a crèche, given the large numbers of children running around enthusing (or not!) about ice sculptures and so forth. There is only self-service and a bar for any parents in need of a vin chaud restorative.

Though technically not a mountain restaurant, Arc 1950's **la casa** (t 0479 075648) has a sun-trapping porch and serves a very good selection of lunchtime food that makes a welcome break from spag bol and sandwiches (➥ arc 1950).

50

The **au pré gourmand** (t 0479 073746) restaurant has both self-service and table-service sections, offering the standard slop along with more refined ideas like veal and rabbit. The terrace isn't great, but the indoor section has a lovely 360° fireplace to keep you amused. In spite of this, and though the food is fine, unless you're a moth you will find yourself better served 10 yards down the snow in the **belliou la fumée** (t 0479 072913). It's a table-service only establishment with a pretty similar menu to Au Pré Gourmand, but all cooked up in far nicer surroundings. Small, cosy and much more private than the Gourmand, though it is difficult to tell if the food is actually better the atmosphere is so superior that it doesn't really matter - they could serve you cereal and you'd probably be happy enough.

From the top of the Aiguille Rouge cable car, almost anywhere on the run down towards Villaroger makes a good spot for a **picnic**. For somewhere a little different, lug your thermos up to the top of the Grand Col chairlift.

getting home

The quickest way back over the ridge depends on when you are - if you're high enough up, ski to the Plagnettes chairlift (or take the Bosses drag). If you are lower down, for instance if you've just finished a lazy afternoon on the terrace of the Chalets de l'Arc restaurant, the best way to get home is to take the Bois de l'Ours lift from under Arc 1950. From the top of that lift you can ski back to anywhere (though to get to Vallandry you may need to do a bit of improvisational traversing).

The slopes above 1600 are a mixture of colours and gradients that present a range of challenges for all levels of skier. There is not as much choice as in other areas and it falls short of Vallandry as a bad weather destination, but much of the skiing is below the tree line - though that gives it a bit of an enclosed feel, it also makes for a very different experience to skiing the wide open areas above 1800 and 2000.

access

You can ski over to the 1600 sector from the top of the Vagère and Carreley chairlifts in 1800, or from the Comborcières and Bois de l'Ours chairlifts below Arc 1950.

pistes

There are more **blue** pistes above 1600 than any other colour, though the majority are low level beginner's runs or tracks to get you to somewhere else. The Mont-Blanc run down from the chair of the same name is a pleasingly wide jaunt through the trees, and higher up the run down from the Clocheret chair is a good introduction to the steeper side of cruising.

Possibly the nastiest **red** in all of Paradiski is found here - the Malgovert accessed from the Comborcières chairlift below Arc 1600 is a winding and at times very narrow track that with poor snow conditions can be almost unskiable. Without room to pick a line through the ledgy bumps, even the best

map c

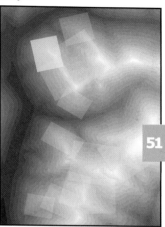

51

---

snapshot

out of interest
highest point - 2418m
aspect - w
pistes - a few blues, fewer reds & 2 tough blacks
off-piste - limited
restaurants - 0

highlights & hotspots
the malgovert red can be a nightmare in poor snow
low slopes are gentle and quiet for beginners
no mountain restaurants, so bring your tupperware

of skiers will be reduced to a spluttering descent. Unless it has snowed recently, you are advised to check the conditions before setting off, as once you're on your way there's not much chance to opt out. The other reds in the area are less challenging and much more pleasant.

The 2 **blacks** - the short Deux Têtes and the considerably longer Rouelles - are hard work without ever being too demanding. The Rouelles (reached from the top of the Cachette chair) is a sustained descent all the way down to the edge of 1600 - though unfortunately the wrong end for you to be able to crash into a bar for a celebratory drink.

52

snowpark

Though technically above 1800, the excellent snowpark is also depicted on the 1600 map (➔ 1800).

off-piste

There's not a lot to speak of, unless you count the largely unpisted black runs. You can pick your way down beside the pistes from the Cachette and Clocheret chairlifts, but you are unlikely to find anything more satisfying than the odd patch of powder alongside the pistes - but at least it's somewhere to steal a few fresh turns.

eating & drinking

The only place to eat is in the resort itself - the nearest mountain restaurants are either over towards 1800 (the Arpette and Altiport) or on the other side of the hill, below Arc 1950 (Au Pré Gourmand and Belliou la Fumée).

There aren't too many attractive options for **picnicking** above 1600 - it's mostly in the trees, and there aren't too many spots with great views. The top of the Clocheret chairlift isn't a bad spot, and for something secluded in the shade take the wide blue piste from the Mont Blanc chairlift and just stop wherever takes your fancy.

getting home

Getting home from 1600 can be a bit of a slow affair. The Gollet or Cachette chairlifts both take you high enough to ski across into the Arc 1800 sector, and the quickest way across the ridge is on the Clocheret chairlift.

The wide open area above Arc 1800 offers some of the best intermediate level pisted skiing to be found anywhere in the Alps. It is difficult to match for sheer volume of reds and blues, and the diversity is sufficient to please most passions. Wide, narrow, steep, gentle, twisty, straight... in addition 1800 is home to Les Arcs' snowpark, and Arc 2000, Vallandry and the Vanoise Express are only a lift away. The only thing missing is peace and quiet - though on quieter weeks towards the end of the season you might even get that.

access

From 2000 the quickest way over is the Bois de l'Ours chairlift. From 1600 take the Cachette or Gollet, and from Peisey-Vallandry find your way to the Plan de l'Ours chairlift.

pistes

Lots of **blues** with plenty of width, though not too much longevity - the area south of the Vagère chairlift is so open and the gradient so even that by halfway down you can basically go wherever you want.

There are oodles of **red** options north of the Vagère - the constant gradient means you can get up high speeds if you straightline or link plenty of turns if you're working on your carving. The unpisted red Clair Blanc run from the top of the Col des Frettes chairlift is a brief but satisfying mogul descent. Or if you turn left from the top of the

map d

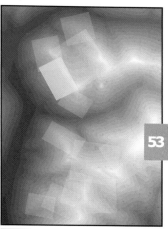

53

snapshot

out of interest
highest point - 2425m
aspect - w
pistes - lots of blues, even more reds & the odd black
off-piste - some
restaurants - 5

highlights & hotspots
lots of pistes
lots of people
paradiski's best snowpark
the always busy arpette restaurant
the always friendly aiguille grive restaurant

lift you get to the area's only **black** run, which is much the same only a little steeper, a little tougher and a little more prone to becoming ledgy.

snowpark

The park above 1800 is basically very good. It has bad points: it is not long (lines of 3 jumps), its lift is a slow 2-man chair, and the bottom of the park issomehow constantly busy with people who shouldn't be there (skiers traversing from the top of the Cachette or Gollet chairlifts wind up in the exit to the park). But the jumps are well maintained, the lift will be replaced for the 2005/2006 winter season and the 3 difficulty levels are well pitched for beginners, intermediates and experts (in jumping terms). There are rails and a table, though it can be difficult to get a decent run-in to the beginner's rail because the hangout point is just in front of it. It can be a struggle to get enough speed up for the first hit of the black line too... but these are minor points. It's better than anything in La Plagne, so much so that many seasonnaires come over from the other side of the valley to work on their gnarliness.

54

off-piste

Almost all of the skiable area is pisted - you can drop off the ridgeline north of the Grive (though beware of rocks if there's only a thin covering of fresh snow). Lower down you're unlikely to find much apart from piste-side powder.

eating & drinking

With long tables, benches, and a noisy snake of a line queuing up for food, **l'arpette** (t 0479 074580) is much the same as a school dining hall - but at the same time it is the best self-service restaurant in Les Arcs. There is an enormous range of food, all of which is promoted in plastic laminated photos above the long counter - so non-French speakers can just point at what they want and smile sweetly. Most of the dishes are good, and the enormous hall could fit more or less every skier on the mountain. The restaurant section has a lovely 360° fireplace, the front terrace is huge and the back one with the sun-loungers is often reasonably quiet. There's a separate bar if all you want to do is drink, and if the queue's too long there's a waffle stand for high speed food. And in addition to all this, the Arpette offers a weekly evening meal and torchlit descent (by reservation). Though this sounds civilised and nice, it isn't - the usually impressive turnout is mainly from the younger generation, and more often than not the misleadingly gentle 5pm vin chaud transforms into a degenerate table-dancing party by 10pm. You'll be back in 1800 by 11pm - just in time for a high-speed shower before steaming your way to Apokalypse.

Just down from the Snowpark, **l'altiport** is a cool place that is effectively just a burger shack. The tiny service window means you'll probably have to queue for a bit, and seating is mostly outside so you're stuffed if it's snowing. But you can buy vin chaud by the litre, and they have a sound system, so this is a great place to get your party started - and non-smokers can sit indoors under an unusual curved glass roof.

l'aiguille grive (t 0479 074397) is split between 2 levels. Downstairs is a warm and friendly snack bar, and is a popular espresso stop for many ESF instructors. Upstairs is the table service version, offering set-price menus alongside steaks and salads and so on.

The last of the hillside choices is the **blanche murée** (t 0609 405653), a pleasant and friendly place down to the right from the Transarc mid-station.

The best and least used spot for a **picnic** luncheon from your backpack is the top of the Grand Renard chairlift.

You get a great view of the Aiguille Rouge and down towards Arc 1950, and very few people take the chair so you're unlike to have to fight for a bit of snow to sit on.

getting home

Any number of lifts will take you across the ridge to the Aiguille Rouge sector. If you're down in the resort, your choice depends on the queues - in practice it is usually quicker to take the Villards chairlift and then the Grand Renard, but if it's cold and you'd rather take a direct trip, the Transarc takes you all the way over the ridge.

Superb tree skiing, some good beginners' areas and excellent access make up Vallandry's ski area. Now also home to the Vanoise Express, there are new lifts and restaurants springing up to provide for what is at times a considerable volume of traffic. But other attractions of the area are often overlooked - many of those passing through are doing just that - using the area to get to somewhere else. As a result, the tree-skiing isn't tracked out too quickly after a snowfall, the pistes are rarely too crowded and there are dividers on the piste that section off the beginner's spots, so learner skiers aren't likely to feel swamped by high speed passers-by.

56

access
From 1800 you can ski into Vallandry from pretty much anywhere.

pistes
Although Les Arcs doesn't do **green**, the main Vallandry and Peisey lifts lead to designated beginner's areas which are shielded from the rest of the pistes.

Not many **blues** to speak of, though there are some decent cruises. The most notable blue is the Forêt track, that runs from the top of the Vallandry chairlift all the way down to the Vallandry village. It crosses other steeper pistes with frightening regularity, and it is so flat that there is plenty of poling and boarders may have to unstrap - but for those who like a

map e

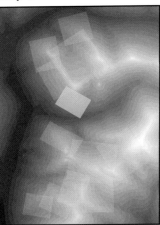

snapshot

out of interest
highest point - 2335m
aspect - sw
pistes - wiggly & mostly flat blues, lots of reds & 2 blacks - 1 short, 1 long
off-piste - trees
restaurants - 3

highlights & hotspots
tree-skiing
the vanoise express
tree-skiing
the many crossings of the forêt track

leisurely pace it is the 'downhill' equivalent of a country walk after a Sunday roast.

There are a number of **red** options, none of which are very remarkable. The red down to the Combe draglift is often quieter than elsewhere, thanks to being tucked away in the corner and also because the drag is a little tiresome and *difficile*.

There are 2 **blacks**. The one from the top of the 2300 charlift (which takes you, amazingly, to 2300m), runs its merry way right down to Plan-Peisey and the Vanoise Express, which makes it quite a long drop and an exhilirating or tiring ski, depending upon your energy levels.

off-piste

Vallandry is a heaven for combat skiing. Almost every gap in the trees can be skied, and if you're good at quick turns you will find endless amusement - the gradient is perfect for winding your way down without picking up too much speed and without any surprising drop-offs. A little higher up and over towards 1800, the Plan Bois chair also leads to some interesting opportunities.

eating & drinking

At the top of the old village and only accessible from 1 piste, **le caverne** (t 0479 075002) is a welcome addition to the lunchtime options in Vallandry. Not many people know it's there, apart

from those who are staying there - it is the restaurant part of accommodation run by an English tour operator. That means you'll be served (mostly) English food by (mostly) English waiters, and surrounded by (mostly) English people, so if you're (mostly) fed up of foreign accents this is a good place to hide.

One of the better mountain restaurants in Les Arcs, **la poudreuse** (t 0479 079025) is a big place with a big menu. The food is self-service but drinks are provided by jolly and efficient waiters. Along with steaks and snacks a particular attraction is the *plat du jour* which here is proper food rather than something slopped out of a vat of lentils and offcuts.

There are various **picnic** benches dotted around the area - any of which make sitting down to eat a little more comfortable. The spot which leaves you with the most après-lunch options is the top of the Plan Bois chairlift, from where you can head back towards Vallandry or down towards Arc 1800.

getting home

Both the Vallandry chairlift, the Plan-Peisey chairlift, and the new Grizzli chairlift all take you high enough to ski over to Arc 1800. To get back to the Aiguille Rouge sector you can then take the Plan de l'Ours followed by the Grand Renard (both chairlifts), or ski down into Arc 1800 and take the Transarc.

57

montchavin

Along with being home to the Vanoise Express, the Montchavin-les Coches area has a great deal to offer in its own right. The lower section is the best bad-weather hideout in La Plagne, the upper section catches a lot of sun and has a lot of wide open space. There's a small but well serviced snowpark, and some excellent mountain restaurants. Also, being a little way away from the centre of the ski area, it tends to be a little less busy than the hive that is Plagne Centre.

access

The Vanoise Express (from Plan-Peisey) takes you over to just above Les Coches and Montchavin.

pistes

More of a warning than a highlight, the **blue** track that leads from the bottom of the Chalet du Friolin into the Montchavin area is entirely flat and far longer than you might expect. Boarders will be walking within a minute of setting off, and still walking 20 minutes later. Don't drop into the trees below the piste, because you will quickly come to a steep gorge and you'll just have to hike back up again.

The **red** pistes in Montchavin are mostly shortish runs between the various blues. The best of the runs is the Lac Noir, a shot down through the trees above Les Coches. Be aware that the Esselet run leads to the very flat Bauches track, and even skiers are likely to end up poling

map f

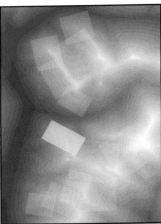

snapshot

out of interest
highest point - 2340m
aspect - ne
pistes - extensive & varied blues, standard reds & 1 black
off-piste - trees
restaurants - 7

highlights & hotspots
the vanoise express
a glut of lovely mountain restaurants
great views over to vallandry
the longest flat track in the world
(➥ pistes)
tree-skiing for cloudy days

(and snowboarders walking) some of the way round to Montchavin.

The Pierre Blanches is the only **black** in the area, and is steep and occasionally bumpy but is nothing out of the ordinary as black runs go.

off-piste

Being largely below the tree line, the Montchavin area is a superb bad weather and tree-skiing destination (if you can get across the Vanoise Express). The terrain is very uneven in places, which can make for some interesting descents, but almost the entire area can be skied if you have the ability.

snowpark

Montchavin's park is probably the best of La Plagne's offerings - it has a boardercross course of sorts, lines of intermediate level kickers and a variety of rails, but its main attraction is its lift access. The Plan Leschaux draglift gets you back to the top in just 4 minutes.

eating & drinking

Spelled variously with and without the 'h', **le christal des neiges** (t 0611 020538) is very large and very prominent. It's easy to get to and a lot of traffic passes it by, so if you want a big terrace where you can work on your tan and show off your new shades, this is your place. If you have any motive other than posing, the Christal has little to recommend it when you could ski 200 yards down to the Plein Soleil. No complaints - apart from slightly pricey food - but it's not as good as the competition.

le plein soleil (t 0673 728755) is a splendid and relatively small restaurant which suffers (or benefits?) from being a bit out of the way. There are assorted signs around the pistes advertising its existence. Follow them. While in reality it's just another mountain restaurant and much like any other, it is run efficiently and well, the menu has a variety of foods from various regions (including sweet and savoury strudels and flammekuche) and it is surprisingly inexpensive.

A little off the pisted track, **chez laurette's** clientele is more cross-country than downhill - to rejoin the marked runs you have to take a short stretch of narrow cross-country piste. The menu is sausages and stews along with typical snacks and a plat du jour. It is a small place and is far enough out of the way to stay pretty quiet.

At the top of the montchavin chair, **le sauget** (t 0479 073851) is a lovely and very homely place with an open fire and decoration that makes you feel like you've walked into someone's house - which in fact you have. It offers accommodation as well as food, and everything is done with great attention to providing good quality service. It is not huge, the menu is not extensive, and the food is not the cheapest around but Le Sauget is cosiness defined.

60

Right next to the Vanoise Express, **le joli bois** (t 0479 074877) is a decent place to sit and look at Les Arcs over a vin chaud. The menu is limited to snacks, crêpes and the odd steak - but the terrace has a great panorama.

les pierres blanches (t 0621 164501) at the top of the chairlift of the same name and the bottom of the snowpark, has nothing out of the ordinary on the menu - omelettes and snacks, tartes for pudding, all in the normal self-service fashion. It does have a big terrace and a bar inside.

Being mostly below the tree-line means there aren't too many **picnic** spots with great views. The top of the Dos Rond chair is fine, but perhaps the best spot is to the right of the last kicker in the snowpark - you don't need to do any jumping to get there, and you can set up shop in the sunshine and watch the talent on display.

getting home

To get back to Les Arcs, take the Vanoise Express from just above Les Coches and Montchavin. If you are low down, the Montchavin chairlift takes you high enough to ski to the cable car.

The area that extends to the south and west above Plagne Bellecôte and Belle Plagne has a broad variety of options and is large enough to keep you engaged for a long time. There are plenty of long descents, some decent mogul runs and good powder access - though also in places some flat sections that will leave boarders cursing and skiers poling.

access

Coming from Les Arcs and hence from Montchavin after the Vanoise Express, there are a number of ways into the Roche de Mio area, and the brand new Bijolin and La Salla chairlifts make access much more swift. The most direct route to the Roche de Mio itself is on the Inversens chairlift.

pistes

For a gentle reintroduction on the first day, the **blue** runs under the Arpette chairlift are an unthreatening cruise that is perfect for getting the parallels going - though boarders may find some sections too flat.

The **red** Clapet run from the Roche de Mio down to the Inversens chair is an excellent piste with a sustained gradient and enough width for you to keep your turns going all the way from top to bottom. And with the Crozats run that follows on and runs down to Les Bauches and the Chalet du Friolin, you can enjoy a 900m vertical drop that ends with an excellent lunch.

map g

61

---

snapshot

out of interest

highest point - 2739m

aspect - w, n, e

pistes - extensive & varied blues (flat in places) & a variety of reds

off-piste - open

restaurants - 6

highlights & hotspots

the excellent clapet red under the inversens chair

the fun moguls off the side of the clapet red

the sources red is a nightmare in poor snow conditions

the uphill tunnel des inversens

off-piste

For mogul hunters, the area directly under the Inversens chairlift usually has the best conditions. Some low level powder can be found under the Bauches chairlift, and there are a variety of places where nipping off the piste can lead to a few fresh turns. Hikers will find a range of runs south of the Roche de Mio, and advanced off-piste skiers are kept happy by the challenging lines down into the Glacier sector.

62

eating & drinking

Over the back towards Champagny, **les quillis** (t 0698 225209) is a large sun-trap crêperie with plenty of space on the 2 level indoor section for when the weather gets bad. It doesn't have the great view of some other places, but the enormous range of sweet and savoury crêpes is compensation enough.

la roche de mio (t 0479 092977) is a very popular place, by virtue of being at the top of 3 lifts and right next to the Glacier access (and there's no mountain restaurant on the Glacier). It's over-priced, over-busy, and in a nod to the Espace Killy you have to pay for the toilets - but if you like the bustling feel of about 4 million sun-loungers on the terrace, this is for you.

A few hundred yards below the Roche de Mio, **les inversens** (t 0609 944378) boasts a fine terrace with arguably the best view in the La Plagne area. Though there is no proper restaurant, the snack food is better value than higher up in the Roche de Mio.

l'arpette (t 0479 091540) is a pleasant building with a decent view over the top of Belle Plagne to the Grande Rochette. Nothing surprising, but service is good and it's generally a much less busy place than the restaurants around the Roche de Mio.

With a nice wooden interior, friendly ownership and warm welcome feel, **le chalet du friolin** (t 0479 074584) is one of the best all-round restaurants you will find in La Plagne. Food is inexpensive and good, they cope well with large groups, and the Friolin has 5 en-suite rooms available on a half-board basis if you want to stay truly in the middle of nowhere. The comfy rooms and intimate night-time meals make for a very different experience to staying in a resort.

le carroley (t 0684 753399) has a stone floor, which gives it a rather different feel inside to many mountain restaurants. The menu is largely made up of simple snacky type food: omelettes, sausages, a plat du jour - along with an excellent homemade quiche. The inside section has 2 levels and you can get table service, though the menu is the same. Outside there is a very large terrace which can be very very busy when it's warm and sunny, thanks to the view and to the lack of other options.

There's plenty of space at the top of the Roche de Mio for a **picnic**, but for a secluded meal try your luck on the Sources red piste - it twists and turns and often has mediocre snow conditions - so you shouldn't have to share your lunch spot with too many others.

getting home
To get back to the Vanoise Express you need to get high enough to ski around the corner of the mountain. Though there is a track from the bottom of the Bauches chairlift, by the Chalet du Friolin, it is very flat. It is much more time efficient (and less tiring!) to take a chair up higher and ski down - the Vanoise Express is well signposted.

When there's a fresh layer of snow on the ground, this is the place people go. Being higher than most areas means more and better sustained snow, so conditions are generally lovely on the few pistes - but the point of the Glacier sector is the enormous off piste potential. It is the launching point for the Bellecôte Glacier off-piste run, and the vast majority of the area is ski-able when there's good snow. Access isn't good, and there are no mountain restaurants, but once you're there you're unlikely to want to stop to eat anyway.

access

There's only 1 way into the area - from the top of the Roche de Mio. You get there either on the Roche de Mio gondola from Bellecôte, from the Inversens chairlift down towards Montchavin. Once you're at the Roche de Mio you take the two-stage Bellecôte gondola into the glacier sector.

pistes

There's not much point in going here to ski on-piste - limited variety means you will be repeating runs within an hour of starting - though because most people will be looking for fresh tracks it doesn't get too busy. Snow conditions this high up are generally very good, and the **blue** runs on the Glacier are wide and pleasant, though relatively short. The **reds** are longer, and the 'Chiaupe' run is challenging, particularly in the unpisted top section. The **blacks** are all off-piste.

map h

snapshot

out of interest
highest point - 3266m
aspect - w
pistes - short blues, 2 long reds & off-piste blacks
off-piste - open, extensive
restaurants - 0

highlights & hotspots
no restaurants
difficult to access
difficult to leave
great off-piste potential
la face nord du bellecôte
glacier skiing - good on piste snow

off-piste

The Glacier sector offers huge opportunity to find untracked snow. The 2 black runs from the Traversée chair are marked on the official map as pistes but in reality there's nothing more than a vague sign as you leave the red run. After that, you're on your own. Two main traverse lines lead to the other side of the ridge, from where you can choose where you're going and as long as you don't go too far north you'll wind up by the Chalet de Bellecôte chairlift.

This is the launching point for the north face of the Bellecôte. For experts there are also a number of lines off the back of the Roche de Mio that lead down to the Chalet chair, but these are much more treacherous - if you don't know where you're going you may wind up staring down a sheer drop or a rocky section you can't traverse around. Don't go without a guide.

eating & drinking

picnic, or nowt. Pretty much anywhere you like can serve as a spot to sit on the snow and stuff down a sandwich. A reasonably quiet option is the space just below the top of the Chalet de Bellecôte chairlift.

getting home

The only official way back is by lift (the Bellecôte gondola), which closes relatively early even in late season. From the bottom of the Chalet de Bellecôte chairlift you can in theory ski all the way back to the Vanoise - making your way down to the Bauches chairlift at the far extent of the Roche de Mio area - but you're off-piste for most of the way and the descent isn't very exciting, and has flat sections especially towards the end that will not amuse a tired snowboarder. You are better off taking a lift to get you higher up before turning for home. Then of course from Montchavin you need the Vanoise Express.

65

Though not the largest of areas, Champagny has more variety and fewer people than most other sectors. There is a misguided sense among some skiers of it being a little bit 'around the corner', but in fact it is easily accessed and all ability levels are catered for: there are gentle cruises, steady red runs, a bumpy black and a decent (though poorly accessed) snowpark. Throw the Roc de Blanchets restaurant into the mix and you have all the ingredients of a fine day's skiing.

66

access

There are 2 good routes from the Vanoise Express - you could either head up to the Roche de Mio on the Inversens charlift and then ski down, or take the La Salla chairlift and ski over to Plagne Bellecôte, then take the Blanchets chairlift.

pistes

Perhaps the longest cruise in La Plagne is the **blue** Geisha track, which runs from the top of the Grande Rochette all the way to the Verdons Sud lift. The top section can only be accessed by the Funiplagne gondola in Plagne Centre, or you can join the piste lower down.

The oriental-sounding Kamikaze and Hara-Kei **reds** are both excellent and sustained descents. Both are accessed by the Verdons Sud chairlift. They catch a lot of sun, and in warmer late season weather both are prone to afternoon closure if the snowpack is unstable.

map i

snapshot

out of interest
highest point - 2450m
aspect - s, w
pistes - cruisey blues, a couple of fast reds & a bumpy black
off-piste - limited, open
restaurants - 3

highlights & hotspots
something for everyone
the roc de blanchets restaurant
one of la plagne's longest (blue) cruises
snow runs out on the pistes down to the village

In between the 2 red runs is Les Bosses, a marked but ungroomed **black** run that - as the name suggests - is La Plagne's best bumps run. It is steep all the way and though not as challenging as the bumps above Arc 2000 on the other side of the Vanoise Express, it will put you through your paces and has the advantage of being flanked by easier pistes if it all gets too much.

off-piste

The majority of the Champagny sector has limited off-piste potential - aside from the little sections between the pistes and the ridge that runs parallel with the Rossa chair, the only real place to find powder is from the summit of the Grande Rochette (which can only be accessed from the Plagne Centre sector). Terrain there is very uneven and often remains untracked in spots long after a snowfall. If you are coming back from skiing the Cul de Nant you rejoin the ski area in Champagny.

snowpark

If it had a lift, the Champagny park would be the best in La Plagne. You can pick from a number of lines, various rails, and lines of kickers colour-coded for their difficulty. Landings off the kickers are mostly quite steep. As with all parks be aware that it will be closed in early morning while maintenance is carried out - this tends to be something of a rolling process here, with different sections being closed at different times during the day. The glaring problem is

that without hiking back up after each run, you have to go all the way down to the Rossa chairlift to loop around.

eating & drinking

At the southernmost extent of Paradiski, **le roc de blanchets** (t 0479 082993) is one of the best restaurants on the La Plagne side. The self-service section is much the same as anywhere else, but the restaurant offers a range of Savoyarde specialities, including a lunchtime fondue. And if it's sunny, there's a south-facing terrace which has a view that extends over to the Courchevel altiport.

67

On the track that joins the Verdons Sud and Borseliers lifts, **les borseliers** (t 0607 549619) is a multi-level chalet building that offers a snacky menu in the 'sausage & chips' vein along with a range of crêpes and galettes. It's a friendly place with a bar, a non-smoking room, and a south facing terrace.

The benches at the top of the snowpark are ideal for a **picnic** - though seeing a big crash may put you off your food.

getting home

The quickest route back to the Vanoise is the Quillis chairlift, from where you can get to Plagne Bellecôte and the Arpette chair, which takes you high enough to get home. From Bellecôte the route is well signposted along the sides of the pistes.

plagne centre

La Plagne's main hub is a criss-cross melange of blue and red, with some very unusual terrain and almost as many lifts as pistes. If it weren't for all the skiers, the extraordinary undulations could make you feel like you're on the moon. As it is, the skiing around Plagne Centre is ample for beginners, intermediates and lunch lovers - though there is nothing particularly challenging in the whole area, it is perfect for cruising.

access

To access the skiing above Plagne Centre you have to make your way through Plagne Bellecôte - the best route is on the La Salla chairlift and then a ski down. From Bellecôte the quickest route over to Centre is on the Colosses chairlift.

pistes

True to the family orientation of the resort, much of the central blend of pistes is **blue** - gentle, and spacious enough to accommodate both ski school lessons and other skiers without too much problem. Though it may look confusing on the piste map, almost all runs lead to Centre, from where it is easy to get back up the mountain.

Of the **reds** on offer perhaps the most interesting is the run under the Colorado chair, which although neither long particularly difficult takes you down through Centre's unusual scenery. The longest and fastest red is the Véga run

map j

snapshot

out of interest
highest point - 2508m
aspect - nw
pistes - a variety of blues & a handful of reds
off-piste - limited
restaurants - 4

highlights & hotspots
family friendly
funky terrain
nothing harder than a red
the véga chairlift is really slow
indoor picnic room

from the top of the Grande Rochette. And that's as hard as it gets as there are no **blacks**.

off-piste

There are a number of very steep and very narrow couloirs straight down under the Funiplagne, but for mortals they are as good as unskiable. Most of everywhere you can get a piste basher is a piste of some description, so if you're looking for fresh tracks you are better off somewhere else.

snowpark

Above Plagne Bellecôte there is both park, big air jump and halfpipe. The pipe and big air is served by the Colosses draglift, though you can easily hike up between runs. Bellecôte's once disappointing snowpark has been newly refurbished for winter 2004-2005.

eating & drinking

Just above Plagne Soleil, the **dou de praz** (t 0479 090540) is notable for offering table service. The interior is pleasant but small, and on sunny days there's a good-sized terrace where you can enjoy your crêpes and snacks.

Over towards Plagne Bellecôte, the **chalet de la trieuse** (t 0479 090258) is a self-service restaurant with a nice feel to it - due in the main to its well varnished finish. The ample terrace space and a relaxed atmosphere make it a pleasant place for long lunch - though keep an eye on the clock.

la bergerie (t 0479 090795) is a plat du jour sort of affair at the crossroads above Plagne Villages. Nothing unusual on the menu, but there is table service, a lovely stone-walled interior and a terrace on which to while away the lunch hour.

The top of the Funiplagne ought to be the perfect place for a large and good restaurant. Unfortunately the **grande rochette** (t 0479 090908) is neither - the menu is very normal, and the service leaves a little to be desired. Not a bad restaurant, but a mediocre one.

69

The best **picnic** spot is the top of the Grande Rochette, where you can soak up the lunchtime sun happy in the knowledge that you're spending less and eating better than the souls in the Grande Rochette behind you. If you want somewhere more official, there's a huge *salle hors-sac* (a picnic room) by the bottom of the Mélèzes chairlift.

getting home

From Centre take the Mélèzes chairlift, from where you can ski down to Plagne Bellecôte and the Arpette charlift which leads over towards Montchavin. The Vanoise Express is well signposted both at the lifts and at the side of pistes.

West of Plagne Centre, the immediate area around Aime la Plagne is a relatively small group of pistes leading down to Centre and Plagne 1800 - but a little further out towards Montalbert, there are also some challenging ungroomed runs which are less skied than almost any other part of La Plagne.

access

Getting to Aime la Plagne is a bit of a journey - it will probably take you an hour or so from the Vanoise Express to get to the resort itself. Head to Plagne Bellecôte, then take the Colosses chairlift and ski down to Centre, then up on the Becoin.

70

pistes

Much of the mish-mash between Aime la Plagne and Plagne Centre is **blue**. It is pretty standard stuff all round - the longest and most interesting cruise in the area is the Gavotte piste from the top of the Crêtes draglift down to Plagne Centre.

The 2 **reds** from the top of the Becoin chairlift are steady descents which catch a lot of sun - and which are thus prone to getting very slushy in late season. The notable red of the area is the 'Emile Allais', which leads down from under the Golf chairlift. Perhaps because of the *'Téléski Difficile'* signs at the top, it is generally very quiet, and if you want the chance to straightline without having to weave around slower skiers, this is a good place to do it. Be warned

map k

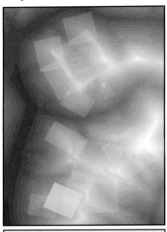

le biollet is a simple snack-on-the-terrace place. There are more 'Pique-Nique Interdit' signs than there are choices on the menu - but if it's sunny and you're hungry, it's as good a place as any - and the view down to Plagne Centrale and across to the Grande Rochette gives you plenty to look at.

A shortish slide down from Aime la Plagne is one of La Plagne's little secrets - **aux bon vieux temps** (t 0479 092057) is a lovely and tiny restaurant that serves a range of Savoyarde specialities for lunch by the piste. Food is excellent, but the reason to go is the atmosphere, which is wonderfully intimate and very different to the restaurants in Aime la Plagne proper.

71

though, the draglift back up is indeed 'difficile'.

The variety of ungroomed **black** runs over the ridge towards Montalbert make up some of the most difficult skiing in La Plagne. They are the steepest and most technically demanding descents away from the Glacier sector, and though fresh snow draws crowds of powder hunters, in sunny weeks the often poor conditions on these runs mean they are generally quite quiet.

For **picnics**, there is a spot with an impressive panorama at the top of the Crêtes draglift, which makes a pleasant and quite airy place to munch your lunch.

getting home

Getting back is much the reverse of getting there - you have to pass through Plagne Centre, from where you want the Mélèzes chairlift, down to Bellecôte and then over on the Arpette chairlift. There are plenty of signs to the Vanoise Express so you shouldn't get lost.

off-piste
On the western side of the ridge above Aime la Plagne is an expanse of mostly skiable, ungroomed terrain - though it cannot be classed as true 'off-piste' as the main lines are marked as black runs. There is very little other off-piste in the area.

eating & drinking
At the top of the lift of the same name,

montalbert

The most inaccessible sector of La Plagne's skiing, the area above Plagne Montalbert is a good destination for beginners - though those staying on the other side of the Vanoise Express will struggle to get there. More capable skiers who do get there will probably only have time to down a quick vin chaud in the Skanapia and then head back again - as Montalbert is as far from Les Arcs as you can get. However if you can make speed of the essence the unthreatening and tree-lined slopes are enjoyable. There's not much variety of gradient, but it's a good place to escape the crowds. In late season the low level makes the snow disappear fast, and this sector will be slushy long before the higher areas.

72

access

From Plagne Centre there are 2 options - either take the Becoin chairlift to above Aime la Plagne and head down to the Adrets chairlift, or ski down to Plagne 1800 and take the 1800 chairlift up, then ski down to the Adrets chair. If you have time, you can ski all the way down to Montalbert rather than taking the Adrets lift, but the track is lengthy and gets pretty flat, so it isn't advised for boarders or for skiers in a rush.

pistes

No **greens** really, though the area just above the village is open and gentle. **blue** is the operative colour. The reds might as well be blue too - everything

map I

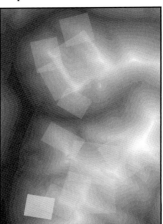

snapshot

out of interest
highest point - m
aspect - w, n, e
pistes - lots of gentle blues & a few gentle reds
off-piste - limited
restaurants - 3

highlights & hotspots
out of the way
in the trees
lots of gentle runs
too many flat runs for boarders
snow disappears fast in late season
not many spots for lunch

above Montalbert is relatively gentle. The straight descent from the top of the Fornelet chairlift down to the village is a decent ski and will work off the calories you put on during your picnic at the top.

There are a couple of **reds** down through the trees, but the red of note is over towards the Adrets chairlift on the edge of the sector. It starts off frustratingly flat, but when you get to the drop it is pleasingly steep for a short while - the only place around Montalbert where an intermediate might feel a little scared. Especially as there are no **blacks**.

off-piste
Despite the forests Montalbert is not really the place for tree skiing, though it can be done in places. There is limited potential for powder, as the sector is significantly lower than most of La Plagne and so gets less snow and loses it faster.

eating & drinking
The **thé menthe** and **skanapia** are technically in Montalbert village and so are not really mountain restaurants, but they see a lot more action at lunchtime than in the evenings. The only spot on the pistes for is the **forpêret** (t 0479 555127).

The flat area at the top of the Fornelet chair would be an ideal spot for a restaurant - as it is there's little more than a bench or two, which makes it a good spot to unwrap the tinfoil and tuck into your baguette.

73

getting home
Coming home you have to make your way back to above Aime la Plagne - from the top of the Fornelet chairlift ski down to the Coqs chairlift, which takes you high enough to ski directly down to Plagne Centre. Then the Mélèzes chairlift, ski down to Bellecôte, take the Arpette chairlift, and then make your way over to the Vanoise. Bon Courage!

So many pistes, so little time. Often it's difficult to know where to start, where to find the longest runs, or where to go when there's not much snow or the weather is bad. Here are a few suggestions.

legs back

Though there are blues and reds to be found all around the area, there is something relaxing about skiing among trees that makes both Villaroger and Vallandry great locations to ease yourself back into your parallel turns. Both have restaurants enough for coffee and food stops, and being at the two extents of the Les Arcs area you are likely to find the slopes less busy than those around 1800 and 2000, and less filled with families and beginners than those above 1600.

all-day sunshine

If it's time to tan, you can track the sun from first light to last. Spend the morning in the Villaroger sector, whose view of our star is unimpeded by steep ridges. Coffee at the Solliet before heading over to 2000 for the midday rays and lunch on any of the many terraces. If you can sum up the energy to move from your lounger, after 3pm you are better off on the 1800 side, and whether your taste is for the piste or the park you can potter your way to the perfect bronze right up until the last lift home.

a long lunch

Les Arcs has plenty of options for quality eating on the mountainside. Though not in the same league as Zermatt, the full gamut of options is available. At some places (like the Altiport and Arpette) your lunch will be long partly because you will have to stand in a queue - for the perfect lazy *dejeuner* head either to Les Chalets de L'Arc for great food and great service, or to the snowpark, where if you take your own sandwiches you can chill on the benches all afternoon while listening to music and watching the grace or otherwise of people going off the jumps.

the paradiski tour

There are people who's life's passion it is to travel to every tube station on the Underground in the shortest possible time. The Vanoise Express opens up a similar possibility for skiers - though there's no way you could take every

74

Paradiski lift in a day, if you plan carefully it is possible to visit every resort in Les Arcs and La Plagne in the space between first lift and last. Tell us your route and your best time by sending them to comments@snowmole.com.

a bumpy ride

There is no shortage of moguls in Les Arcs. For an all day play, warm up on the gentle red down from the Arpette chair. Once your legs are going, head down the other side of the ridge under the Bois de l'Ours chair, which is black and a bit more challenging. From there you have options: either head up the Marmottes chair and then take the Varet gondola to access the pleasures of the Aiguille Rouge, or to avoid the crowds head over to 2000 and then up the Lanchettes chairlift. Left from the top of the Lanchettes leads you to perhaps the least-skied mogul run in the area - an unpisted black that takes

you down towards the Comborcières chair (and the excellent Belliou La Fumée restaurant if you need a restorative!). Whichever order you ski the bumps, be kind to your knees - you'll miss them when they're gone.

bad weather

Cloud cover and heavy snowfall are no obstacle to great skiing. Whether you want to be in the thick of the trees or on the pistes in between them, the forested area above Peisey-Vallandry offers oodles of opportunity for exercise when you can't see where you're going in the other sectors. If that's too far away or you can't get there because of lift-closures, Villaroger also has enough trees to keep the clouds away.

cross the valley

There are any number of reasons to take the trip across to La Plagne. Trainspotters can soak up the stats of the construction while hanging an impressive 400m above the valley floor, food-lovers can munch at one of the many mountain restaurants in and above Montchavin on the other side, explorers have the whole of La Plagne to discover, experts can get to the Bellecôte glacier... and every single person can get rid of some more pesky Euros.

75

Les Arcs is a superb off-piste destination. Piste-side powder-poachers can take their pick - almost every run in the area has open space off to the side. Those that don't tend to have trees, so combat skiers will be more than happy too. Hikers will not find marked itineraries like in Verbier or Zermatt, but hiring a guide will reveal a world of powder trails both well known and not. Ask any local about the best off-piste in the area and you will hear 3 names - the Grive, the Rouge and Bellecôte.

76

l'aiguille grive

At 2732m, L'Aiguille Grive doesn't exactly tower over Les Arcs. What it does do, however, is provide some eminently accessible top level powder skiing. As a result it gets tracked pretty quickly, but if you get there early you will find some excellent lines. The runs are accessed by the Transarc gondola (from 1800) or Plagnettes chair (from above 1950 & 2000). Ignoring the appeal of the Ice Grotto, the hike heads up the ridgeline, where there is likely be a boot track. From the top of the Grive you face a tricky traverse and a nasty (but brief) couloir before picking your line down towards Vallandry. First you reach a series of couloirs. If these don't seem too appealing you can traverse further along to where the face opens out - basically the further you go the easier it becomes. The Grive is best scouted from the Plan Bois chairlift and best skied in the morning (as it is

south-facing and prone to slipping in the afternoon sun). But make no mistake - the Grive is for expert skiers only and should under no circumstances be attempted without a guide.

l'aiguille rouge

If you can put up with the queue (or you can find some way of jumping it), the Aiguille Rouge cable car leads to just under the 3226m summit of the same name - and to a lot of powder potential. Heading straight back down towards Arc 2000 makes for a longish and very open ski - though much of this may be mogulled unless there has been a recent fall. On the other side of the ridge there are a variety of runs that take you down towards Villaroger - though much of this side cannot be skied because it is a designated nature reserve.

la face nord du bellecôte

An extraordinary and very challenging descent that leads straight down the north face of the Bellecôte, Paradiski's highest peak at 3417m. Though the start of the run is over in La Plagne, with the Vanoise Express in place it is easy enough to get to. However even if you start early you won't be there much before 11am as there are plenty of lifts between the Vanoise and the top of the Bellecôte glacier. The main line down is basically very steep at the start, and then very steep all the way down. For those that brave the run and make it to the bottom, the rewards extend even beyond the thrill of the descent. You come out on the cross-country skiing route in the beautiful Vanoise National Park, where you will find the **l'auberge les chabottes** restaurant in Nancroix - the perfect spot to stop for lunch and wait for the bus back to Peisey.

ski touring

There is a whole world of skiing that goes almost unnoticed by the majority of recreational skiers. Those used to

huge, linked ski areas with endless lifts and mile after mile of pisted runs may well not know what ski touring is. It is also called ski mountaineering, which is perhaps a more appropriate name for it - it consists effectively of climbing up mountains before skiing down them. It is quite unlike normal skiing in that it is entirely off-piste, and 'tours' consist of travelling from 'a' to 'b' in the same way as hiking trails in summer. Obviously to make this possible a lot of different equipment is necessary. To climb up slopes with skis on you need touring bindings, which you can unlock to allow your heel to come away from the ski as you step upwards. You also carry 'skins' - so called because they were originally seal skins - which are strips attached to the bottom of the ski during a climb to allow them to slip uphill but prevent them from sliding down. For many tours it is also necessary to be proficient with climbing ropes and harnesses... but if you hire a guide you will be surprised what you can do - and all these delights are available to boarders as well, simply using snowshoes or approach skis when skiers use skins. Though the area is not nearly as extensive as Chamonix or Zermatt, the mountains around Les Arcs offer numerous touring opportunities. If you're tempted the best first step is to talk to a guide (➝ lessons & guiding).

77

In the eventing world Les Arcs is best known for the *Kilometre Lancé*. But there is a diverse range of other competitions, some do with skiing and some of which just need snow.

ski-joëring is like chariot racing on skis, Ben Hur with snow ponies pulling skiers instead of racehorses pulling chariots. Without the big dusty stadium. And without the spiky wheels. And without Charlton Heston. To the un-French, it is a little difficult to take seriously, but it is quite funny and very entertaining. The French Championship is held at the end of January - details from the tourist office.

A snowshoe race, **la vaugelette** is another event that will fill most holidaymakers with amusement or interest rather than adrenalin and envy. It operates pretty much how you would expect, a bit like a cross-country race through the mud. Mid-February's the time, and again the tourist office have the full run down, or rather across.

A little closer to what you might be used to, **la belle fente** is a telemark convention, and spends its time celebrating all things without heel attachments. More like a biker's meet than a competition it's a gathering point for those who have fallen in love with skiing's quirky brother. The 1 day show in Arc 1800 consists of telemarking around the place and generally being sociable, with a demonstration after

lunch and an itinerary that includes an array of evening activites (though these are more about drinking than skiing).

The event that marks Les Arcs on the freeride calendar, the **north face freeride** is a pro-ski contest on a very demanding off-piste course. Competitors are marked on their grace and fluidity relative to their line, meaning that they're trying to look good while skiing stuff that would make the average Joe dissolve into jelly just by looking at it. It all happens over 3 days in early March, weather permitting.

Above Arc 2000 lives the **kilometre lancé** arguably the best speed ski run in the world and the place where the world record was set back in 1999 at just over 248km/h. Both the French and the World Championships take place here every year, late in the season. And both consist of mad people in PVC and a space helmet flying down a slope a little faster than the take-off speed of your Easyjet Airbus.

The snowpark hosts a number of small and locally sponsored events throughout the season, generally aimed at small-name pros and seasonnaires. At the decidedly unofficial end of the scale is the **flying squirrel race**, based out of the bar of the same name in Plan-Peisey, and aimed squarely at the social end of competition. The day long event involves as much drinking as skiing, and fancy dress is obligatory.

78

If you need a break from the downhill grind, there are plenty of other things to keep you entertained on the snow.

If you are very brave or very stupid, you can have a stab at **speed skiing** on the Kilometre Lancé (1800 t 0479 078205, 2000 t 0479 072246) - skiing faster than you would dare to drive (available at certain times through the season). All you have to do it point yourself down the hill and pray. Check before you come out what the grooming schedule is, as if it isn't pisted you're out of luck. When open, it is open to all, and the price includes rental of absurdly long skis and an absurd-looking outfit.

ski-joëring may be what all skiers did before they invented lifts. Or it may not, but either way, it's good silly fun. A comedy pastime that you will never get into properly it's worth a try for the sake of it. Basically you (on skis) get dragged along by a horse. Sadly, board-joëring is not as popular, as the whole process would be rather like taking an awkward draglift. Book through Ranch El Colorado (t 0479 072497).

Subject to the weather, **night-skiing** is on offer Mondays and Tuesdays (until 7pm or 9pm) every week from 1 lift in each of 1600, 1800 and 2000. In early season the skiing is floodlit, but as the days get longer you can simply ski through the sunset. Though the lifts and hence the runs are only short, it is superb fun. Why? Because not a lot of

people do it, so you get plenty of space, you can nurse your hangover in bed until midday and still get a full day on the slopes and because skiing as the sun goes down is like throwing a Frisbee on the beach in summer while someone cooks up burgers on the BBQ.

Illegal in France, you can nonetheless make **heliskiing** drops across the border in Italy. Utterly addictive, in much the same way as ski-touring, you're guaranteed fresh tracks and the incredible feeling of being in the middle of nowhere. Add to that the thrill of travelling by helicopter and you've got quite a package. It's not cheap, but who cares?

If you have any energy left by the evening - or if you want to get rid of the kids for an hour so you can enjoy your hot tub in peace - consider a **quad-bike** (arquad t 0622 566178) or **ski-doo** (ESF or Arc Aventures) excursion. Available above Arc 1800 from the moment the lifts close.

If you can't or don't want to ski **snowshoeing** lets you explore the mountains, and without any danger of hurting your knees or breaking your legs. Snowshoes are like big tennis-rackets, which allow to walk relatively easily over any kind of snow surface while enjoying the calmness of the alps. Book through the ESF, Arc Aventures or Marie-Odile Liothaud (1600 t 0479 071438).

the resort

When you're not on the slopes, how hectic your holiday is depends very much on which resort you are staying in. On the whole Les Arcs is about convenience - what-you-see-is-what-you-get apartments and purpose built commerces - so the resorts have quite a definite pattern about what happens when. There are still some who stay out all night in their ski gear, but away from 1800 this far less common than in resorts like Zermatt or Val d'Isère.

Though there are very few bad **restaurants** in Les Arcs, there are also only a handful that are truly outstanding - and given how separate the different resorts are, you are somewhat restricted in your ability to sample the delights on offer. As Les Arcs is in the Savoie region of France, it is hard to the escape the Savoyarde staple of fondue and raclette. Though most people have the option to cook for themselves, low prices and ski-tiredness mean the restaurants are generally still busy. In part this is due to there not being many of them compared to the number of people in the resorts - so it's a good idea to book a table if you want to eat out. There isn't much of a 'chalet night off' in 1800 or 1600 - as there are few chalets. Only Arc 2000 succumbs to the mid-week fight for restaurant tables - normally Wednesday - when the chalet staff are enjoying their time away from the kitchen sink. A stay in Vallandry, Plan-Peisey or Arc 1950 is somewhat

82

different to the other resorts. At present in 1950 you don't have may choices - though this will change as the resort develops - though the resort club people do charge around trying to make sure everybody is having fun. Vallandry's mass of chalet accommodation makes for quieter times in the restaurants (apart from mid-week) and also for a nightlife that is variable outside of the peak weeks (though the seasonnaire population is generally good at propping up the bar). Throughout the resorts meal prices are reasonable - with a few notable exceptions your fondue will cost and taste much the same wherever you go. In the following reviews the restaurants have a price rating, based on the average price of a main course per head excluding drinks.

£ - under €9
££ - €9-13
£££ - €13-17
££££ - €18-21
£££££ - over €21

The **après** scene is rather unpredictable. In busy weeks everywhere is busy, and though there is generally an early evening lull, if you want a non-stop drinking session you are unlikely to spend any of it alone. Conversely in quiet weeks you struggle to find anyone anywhere. But drinking is much like eating, in that per head of population there isn't much space in the bar, so you may still have to elbow a fellow skier out of the way to get your beer.

snapshot

the best

The ingredients of most people's ideal ski holiday are pretty easy to pin down. You need mountains, and snow, good company, friendly locals, hearty après, stodgy food, some late night revelry and an early morning headache. Accordingly, along with being in the right location, ski resorts tend to provide liberal doses of fondue and beer and let your holiday spirit organise the rest. If you like to go home in the knowledge you've been to the best the area has to offer read on...

The typical Savoyarde experience is best sampled at **chalet bouvier** in Les Villards, the centre of Arc 1800. Also in 1800 **l'équipe** serves up some excellent steak, and **mamie crêpes** offers the best sweet and savoury anywhere on the mountain. If you're staying around the corner in Peisey-Vallandry you have access to 2 excellent and very different restaurants - **l'armoise** in plan-peisey and **l'ancolie** a little further down the hill (but worth making an effort to get to). The **chalet d'arcelle** in Arc 1600 is also a very authentically good restaurant, and in the new Arc 1950 resort **la casa** offers the best Italian food. For something less typical to a ski resort, a funny range of mini-gourmet food is available from **le 4 saisons** in Arc 1800, and also in 1800 the **mountain café** serves up a good tex-mex - along with being a fine and unthreatening place to drink in the après flavour.

83

If you're more concerned with drinking, the most typical English après can be found at the **red hot saloon** in 1800, probably the best place for live music and too much beer, and also the best spot to watch England almost win at football. For a more genuine and friendly English welcome (and in slightly cosier surroundings) the **flying squirrel** in Plan-Peisey is the best spot. Up in Arc 2000 the **crazy fox** is also a fine English hangout - or a little lower down in Arc 1950 **les belles pintes** serves up beer and cheer as it would be like in England if England were how it is perceived to be. There's also plenty of Frenchness around, some of which is a little on the quirky side - the **jo** in 1800 is the best place for live music that isn't so English, and **l'abreuvoir** in 1600 is just rather odd all round. Back in 1800 the **jungle café** is a very French (or Belgian) place to be, and **el latino loco** is Arc 2000's best surprise. For wannabee seasonnaires the best hangouts are **benji's** in 1800 and the **mont blanc** over in Vallandry, and the best of the late night action can be found in 1600, at **café sol** (who run a shuttle bus service through the night between Arc 1800 and their front door).

In general quite a bland place, 1600's non-pizza appeal is limited to a very few establishments: friendly fondue at Les Airelles, homely food at the Chalet de l'Arcelle, quirky après at the Abreuvoir, and buzzy nightlife at Café Sol. The supermarket isn't great, the rental stores are uninspired, and there's very little shopping to be done. You may have one or two quality evenings, but the resort as a whole won't make for too many fond memories.

84   << eating out >>

le chalet de l'arcelle 🟤🟤🟤

p85
e1/2   [1]

☎ 0479 073050
🕐 7pm-10pm
✗ mainly savoyarde

About as hidden away as is possible in such a small resort, the Arcelle is a great little restaurant that has as un-commercial an approach to eating out as you will find anywhere in Les Arcs. The simple room is beautifully decorated and low-lit, and everything about it feels individual. You are more than likely to be served by the owners, who take pride in their presentation of traditional Savoyarde food and a small range of other dishes that are inexpensive given their quality. The neon sign outside is a little off-putting, but even that is

welcome when it's dark and cold and you aren't quite sure how to get to the front door.

les trois ours £

p85
e2   [6]

☎ 0479 077814
🕐 10am-11pm
✗ chips and beer

Sadly, you can't get porridge, nor are there beds or golden-haired girls in the 3 Bears, a more bar than restaurant place at the far end of the commercial walkway. The small TV is on all the time, and if you're someone who likes their dinner on their lap in front of the football, this could be your place - the atmosphere is generally very sociable. The menu includes a kind of 'watch the game' meal of mussels and chips and a beer. Before 7pm there is also a quick snack-style menu.

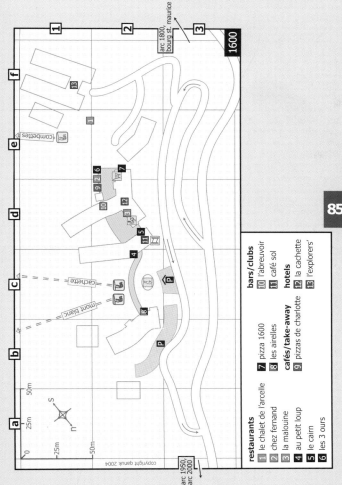

1600

85

restaurants
1 le chalet de l'arcelle
2 chez fernand
3 la malouine
4 au petit loup
5 le cairn
6 les 3 ours

7 pizza 1600
8 les airelles

cafés/take-away
9 pizzas de charlotte

bars/clubs
10 l'abreuvoir
11 café sol

hotels
12 la cachette
13 l'explorers'

arc 1800,
bourg st. maurice

arc 1950,
arc 2000

copyright ganuk 2004

pizza 1600 £

☎ 0479 042773
🕐 6pm-10pm
✗ pizza

Surprisingly, Pizza 1600 is a pizzeria. There is a big choice - of pizza - and the food is far better presented than the restaurant, which would fit quite nicely into a motorway service station. If you aren't into the décor you can take your pizza away and eat it somewhere else - though the service is usually as cheerful as the appearance is cheap, and for the price you could do worse. That said, if you're taking away you can do rather better just around the corner at Pizzas de Charlotte.

86

pizzas de charlotte £

☎ 0479 041884
🕐 6:30pm-10pm
✗ pizza

The best of the deep-pan options in 1600, but very short of seating - it's no Pizza Express, but if you're missing Domino's then head here. There's a pretty big selection of options for toppings and you can pic'n'mix if nothing on the menu takes your fancy. Chicken nuggets and wings and onion rings are also on offer, and if the trip from your apartment is too much to face they do deliver (though not to the Village des Deux Têtes).

le cairn ££

☎ 0479 077985
🕐 10am-10pm
✗ italian & savoyarde

The Cairn is a pleasant and simple restaurant serving typical food at typical prices. Its attraction is the view - but there are limited places by the window, so you would do well to reserve your table in advance and be specific about where you want to sit. You can get pizzas and much of the evening menu at lunchtime, and it has a small terrace and a bar for your post-skiing vin chaud.

au petit loop ££

☎ 0479 077450
🕐 11am-10pm
✗ traditional savoyarde

More restaurant than bar, but with a superb view of the mountains on the other side of Bourg St. Maurice it is as fine a place as you will find for sipping vin chaud as the sun sets. The restaurant gets going at about 7pm - the menu is a limited selection of Savoyarde food that is nothing special but which is at least always accompanied by friendly service.

and the rest

There are 2 other restaurant choices on the 1600 walkway - **la malouine** (t 0479 077459) and **chez fernand** (t 0479 077814). Both offer a pretty standard menu of Savoyarde foods. You will be able to tell by walking past them which one you are best suited to - though if you are looking for something slightly more refined you can also book into the restaurant at the hotel La Cachette, called **la rive** (t 0479 077050).

<< après ski & nightlife >>

les airelles

☎ 0676 918377
🕐 8am-12am
🍴 savoyarde

A spacious wooden affair that is bar, café and restaurant in one. The lunch menu is inexpensive and evenings are Savoyarde in content, operating largely in an all-you-can-eat buffet fashion. Les Airelles is a ceaselessly friendly place that serves equally well as a lunchtime hangout, an afternoon coffee stop, or an evening dining spot. It's a little way from the main part of the resort, which limits its après appeal - but if L'Abreuvoir isn't your cup of tea then Les Airelles is next on the list.

l'abreuvoir

☎ 0479 077050
🕐 4pm-1:30am

1600's only dedicated après bar with an extraordinary combination of furniture and lighting that make you feel you're in a cinema before the film starts - aside

from the disconcertingly angled ceiling and random plants and a variety of odd decorations. If you're not too preoccupied wondering if the décor can be intentional, you can enjoy regular live music, karaoke, video games, table football, and an atmosphere that is as lively as you will find in 1600 until Café Sol gets going around midnight.

café sol

☎ 0479 041341
🕐 5pm-4am

Down the winding stairs, this is the crown of Les Arcs' nightlife, and **87** draws the knowledgeable after-hours crowd from all around the mountain. Though nothing out of the ordinary, the young and lively atmosphere - it is popular with seasonnaires - draws in the punters and it is busy even in quiet weeks. Music can be reggae, trance, drum & bass, and most of what's in between. Entry is free, and between 11pm and 4am Sol runs its own shuttle to 1800 - so for a nominal charge you can experience the Les Arcs' best night spot without having to put up with staying in 1600.

1800

With a far greater degree of choice than the rest of Les Arcs, 1800 is the only resort that will take you more than 5 minutes to explore - and though some of the commerce isn't really worth hunting out, there is diversity enough to cater for most types. Most diners should at some stage make their way to Chalet Bouvier, most drinkers will at some stage be in the Red Hot Saloon, and most clubbers will at some stage find themselves in Apokalypse. For ease of navigation it is nominally divided into 3 sections, with Le Charvet on the left, Les Villards in the middle, and Charmettoger on the right.

<< eating out >>

le choucas £££££

☎ 0479 874225
🕐 7-11pm
✗ traditional savoyarde

p89
a3

Tucked into the corner on the upstairs level of Le Charvet, Le Choucas is a cute and cosy escape from the evening throng. The fondues are good, the *bon acceuil* is more evident here than in some places, and you could go a long way and not find a better steak. Though the range of food is not very far removed from any other Savoyarde restaurant, the way it arrives is better than most places and the restaurant's good reputation is well deserved.

le planté d'baton £££

☎ 0479 074513
🕐 12-3pm, 7m-10pm
✗ traditional savoyarde

p89
a2

What might from the outside appear to be just another Savoyarde place is in fact one of 1800's best restaurants. Excellent from start to finish - on stepping inside you are instantly teleported away from the blandness of the wooden pier, and the food and service are every bit as good as the décor. The menu is creative within the Savoyarde remit, including a mixed grill and a goat's cheese variation on the standard tartiflette... the Baton also offers very cheap pizzas, which are available to eat in or take-away.

89

restaurants
1. le choucas
2. l'équipe
3. le laurus
4. la planté d'baton
5. chez les filles
6. chalet bouvier
7. la cloche à fromage
8. l'équipage
9. le triangle noir
10. le marmite
11. mountain café
12. casa mia

cafés / take-away
13. les 4 saisons
14. mamie crêpes
15. le grenier des arcs
16. le cactus
17. le kebab
18. arc pizza
19. romeo snack
20. SOS pizza

hotels
21. hotel du golf
22. club du soleil

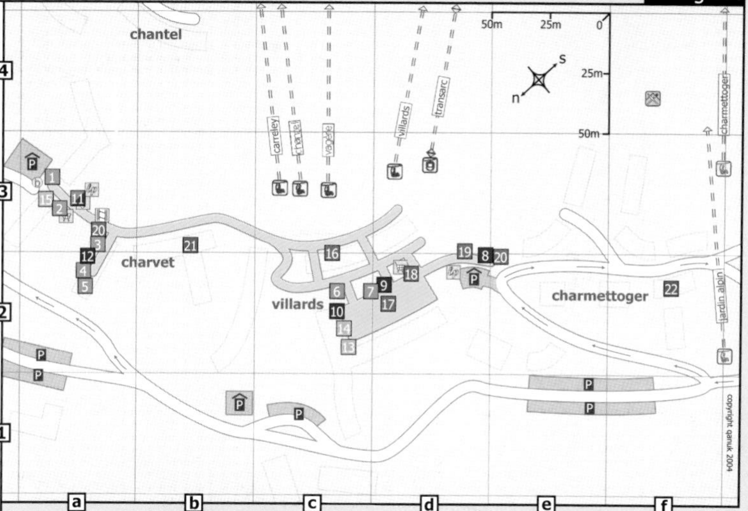

chantel

charvet

villards

charmettoger

copyright qanuk 2004

50m 25m 0 25m 50m

charmettoger

transarc

villards

vaccoto

flache

cartelay

jardin alpin

N S

le 4 saisons £££

☎ -
🕐 8am-8pm
✗ gourmet nibbles

A delicious little tea room tucked away out of range of the window-shopping masses. If you're having a day of pampering, Les 4 Saisons will satisfy your every indulgent whim. You can choose from gourmet style dishes including home-made foie gras, a range of posh omelettes and salads, chocolate fondue, and more teas than you can shake a ski pole at. It is also worth visiting just for the novelty - in a resort without too much true character it has a style all its own, and if you're looking for more unusual presents to take home you can find those here too.

90

chez les filles ££

☎ 0479 041455
🕐 12pm-3pm, 7pm-10pm
✗ traditional savoyarde

At the far extent of the Charvet pier, Chez les Filles is a nice little place which despite the name has no noticeable bias toward the fairer sex. Lunch and dinner follow Savoyarde principles, and the sectioned and largely windowside seating means you can eat without being surrounded by people, and enjoy a view of the snow outside. Its layout means no matter where your table is you never quite feel you're in the central part of the restaurant, but aside from the slightly dislocated feeling there are few complaints to be made.

le triangle noir £££

☎ 0479 077455
🕐 6pm-11pm
✗ savoyarde & duck

A small and excellent restaurant which divides its large menu between souped-up Savoyarde standards and a gourmet range of specialities from France's south west - which basically means lots and lots of duck. Decoration is on the simple side and the à la carte food is not cheap, but if you're watching your wallet there are some less expensive set-price menus and the price tag is not out of place.

casa mia ££

☎ 0479 070575
🕐 12-3pm, 7pm-11pm
✗ italian & pizza

The best of the pizza joints, both for food and for feeling like a restaurant. Casa Mia does a bustling trade and its small size only adds to the cosy busyness - the feu de bois oven turns orders around faster than a Pizza Express and you could be in and out again in 30 minutes if needs be... equally you could while away the best part of the evening in Casa Mia's jolly warmth. There is also a steak-and-chips style menu of other dishes, and the pizzas are available to take away.

le kebab £

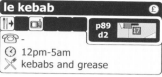

⏰ 12pm-5am
🍴 kebabs and grease

No surprises here. This is the main draw for late night munchers dribbling out of Apokalypse, though it is open almost long enough that early risers (or lost revellers) could have breakfast here. But you won't find croissants on the menu: just burgers, chips, and an elephant leg worthy of any kebaberie back home. And it really is open until 5am.

la cloche à fromages ££

☎ 0479 070854
⏰ 6pm-10pm
🍴 traditional savoyarde

As the name suggests, the Cloche is a haven for all things cheesy. It has no gourmet aspirations, and if you're not a dairy fan you're better off elsewhere - but though it is neither varied in its menu nor particularly attractive in its décor, when it comes to cheese they know their trade. Every dish has a fromage somewhere in the title, and the there's plenty on the menu to keep the choosy eaters happy.

l'équipage £

☎ 0479 071990
⏰ 6pm-12am
🍴 fondue & pizza

Though equally good at catering for groups, L'Equipage is not to be confused with L'Equipe at the other end of the resort. Here you will be served one of the most informal restaurant meals you will eat. The menu is the usual blend of fondue and pizza, and is all much of a muchness - but if you time it right (or you're very persuasive) you will experience the establishment's Hyde side: it is furnished with a healthy set of speakers, tables that are balanced for dancing on, and an owner who is very amenable to people using the microphone for singing practice. Don't go hoping for culinary excellence, but do go expecting to have an enjoyable time.

91

arc pizza ££

☎ -
⏰ 6pm-11pm
🍴 pizza

The best of the take-away pizza places, certainly in terms of variety of choice. They are a little more expensive than elsewhere but it's worth the extra couple of Euros to be able to pick from a 50-strong range that is divided between classic, Savoyarde, seafood, meat, sweet & sour, and some unclassifiable random mélanges. It's not open late, but if your apartment kitchen doesn't seem too appealing after a long day on the slopes then this the perfect no-hassle substitute.

mamie crêperie £ £

☎ 0479 072388

🕐 8am-8pm

✕ crêpes

p89
c2

The Mamie Crêperie is one of the sober delights of Les Arcs. As with much of 1800 it is unremarkable from the outside, and first impressions on entering are simply that it is very small. A group of more than 4 will have to squeeze into their seating, and the utterly inaccessible toilet was clearly designed for a hobbit - but if food matters more than size, this is your place. The crêpes are as good as any in the Alps, the menu is huge and endlessly creative, and the service is so authentically French you could as easily be in Breton.

chalet bouvier £ £ £

☎ 0479 041468

🕐 5pm-11pm

✕ traditional savoyarde

p89
c2

A lovely and refreshingly proper restaurant that takes the sort of care over food and service that every eaterie should. Excellently run, the efficiency and intelligence of the staff give it a very relaxing feel. The adjoining wine bar serves a small but well-picked selection of Savoyarde reds and whites, and the food is equally well thought through and invariably well prepared. Portions are well balanced, the chalet décor is nicely

finished, and the air is more one of authenticity than commerciality. It's quite large and open plan, and so copes as well with groups and families as it does with romantic twosomes - but no matter what your make-up, when you arrive you'll feel welcome and when you leave you'll feel like you want to come back.

and the rest

Other choices include the pleasant and spacious **l'equipe** restaurant (t 0615 892145) and **le laurus** (t 0479 074009) on the pier in Le Charvet, which serve some good Savoyarde dishes. If your evening involves moving between Benji's and the Red Hot Saloon (➥ après-ski & nightlife) you should perhaps eat at the **marmite** (t 0479 074428). Cheap pancake options include a crêpe stand outside the Red Hot Saloon in the afternoons and another outside the Mountain Café - an indoor choice is **le grenier des arcs** in Le Charvet (t 0479 074076). If you're stuck for a snack out towards Charmettoger the nearest is **roméo snack** (t 0479 041541), and from the snow front in Les Villards your best option for a quick lunch snack is **le cactus** (t 0479 071398). If Arc Pizza isn't doing it for you **sos** has 2 outlets - one underneath the stairs at the central end of Le Charvet, the other at the far end of Les Vilards. They are open until 10pm and will also deliver.

<< après ski & nightlife >>

mountain café ££

☎ 0479 070089
🕐 3pm-1am
🍴 tex-mex (& crêpes)

One of the few places where you can escape the all-pervading Savoyarde theme, and one of the best all round spots in all of Les Arcs. At the same time it is a bustling bar and a quality tex-mex restaurant, with a blend of nationalities and an atmosphere that is loud and lively without being too alcohol dependent. Equally good for hot chocolate, coffee, beer, afternoon crêpes or evening burritos and burgers - and as a bar it is relaxed and somehow manages to ward off the macho side of the après scene.

l'ambiente

☎ 0479 074951
🕐 4pm-2am

The Ambiente is a large and largely square place with the bar in the centre of a 3-tiered layout. There's plenty of at-the-bar seating, and 4 TVs mean that - should you want to - you can keep the football in your eyeline no matter where you sit. Expect to hear as much French as English - and expect the TVs to give priority to European games. The atmosphere is at times chilled and at others hectic - loud music and disco lights

ensure a buzzy atmosphere when it's busy, and perhaps a little optimistically there's a chess set for quieter moments.

le gabotte

☎ 0479 074186
🕐 4pm-1am

A very French little watering hole, and *très chaleureux, si vous parlez Français* - but otherwise not the most welcoming of places. You can sit around the square bar and chat to the owner or squat at a table and chat to your friends - either way it's a good pre-dinner drink spot if you're eating on the pier. But don't expect to get away with mumbling your order and then repeating it in English - all you're likely to get in return is the barman mumbling something back at you in French.

93

le 73

☎ 0479 070088
🕐 4pm-2am

You may see fliers around town in which the 73 claims to be a wine bar. These are false. They serve a good vin chaud, but otherwise this is a relatively French blend of everything unrefined. It ought to be a pleasant soirée hangout, but it has set its sights on the cool French seasonnaire crowd - and if you don't fit that bill you may find yourself a little out of sorts. Despite the warm wood furnishing and utter lack of dancefloor, late nights regularly feature live DJing - generally drum & bass or euro-techno - which tends to result in a huddle of brave (or inebriated) souls half-dancing in the doorway. Which for a variety of reasons can make it quite difficult to leave.

red hot saloon

☎ 0479 077452
🕐 11am-2am

Very much 1800's England HQ, the Saloon is very big and mostly very busy. Bar staff are a bit unpredictable, and can be quite surly if they haven't had a good day's boarding, but drinks arrive one way or the other and make no mistake about it, this is a place for drinking. Coffee and hot chocolate are not high on the priority list, but if you want beer and pre-Apokalypse impromptu dancing, this is where to find it. The daily live music is at times quite superb, and the young alcoholic buzz creates as good an après atmosphere as you will find in Les Arcs.

94

la thuria

☎ 0479 074086
🕐 9am-2am

A curious bar that is bizarrely almost never busy in the evenings, La Thuria suffers from a bit of an identity crisis. It very much wants to be a betting shop, but equally it is well disposed to serving coffee and burgers and beer, and with pool and table football getting in the way of things it's hard to know where to look. If you like to waste your Saturday night beer money on random numbers there's a Lotto counter - and if you think afternoons are better spent at the horses than on the slopes, you can spend your week watching the racing on the TVs. And for those who have traded their gambling addiction for French lessons, La Thuria houses plenty of local seasonnaires.

le JO

☎ 0479 074042
🕐 4pm-2am

Advertising itself as a 'live rock café', the J.O. (Jeux Olympiques) is exactly that. They have a projection screen for when there's football on TV, but the emphasis is on live music. The same band plays every night, and has a huge repertoire of songs - some of which you'll recognise, some of which you won't. Evenings tend to be rather two-halved, with everyone studiously avoiding the dancefloor for the first set, and then crowding the same when the band come back on after a beer or two. It's a French place, and the band is French, but many of the songs are in English - which amusingly leads to many of the lyrics being a little off the mark. It all adds to the fun though, and for swing-dancing atmosphere there's nowhere better in 1800.

copyright qanuk 2004

charmettoger

jardin alpin

charmettoger

villards

transarc

cabane

carrelay

crey

villards

charvet

chantel

n

50m   25m

25m

50m

95

bars

1 red hot saloon
2 benji's
3 jungle café
4 before
5 l'ambiente
6 le JO
7 le 73
8 mountain café
9 le cabotte
10 la thuria
11 arc café
12 hotel du golf

clubs

13 apokalypse
14 le fair way
15 sing island

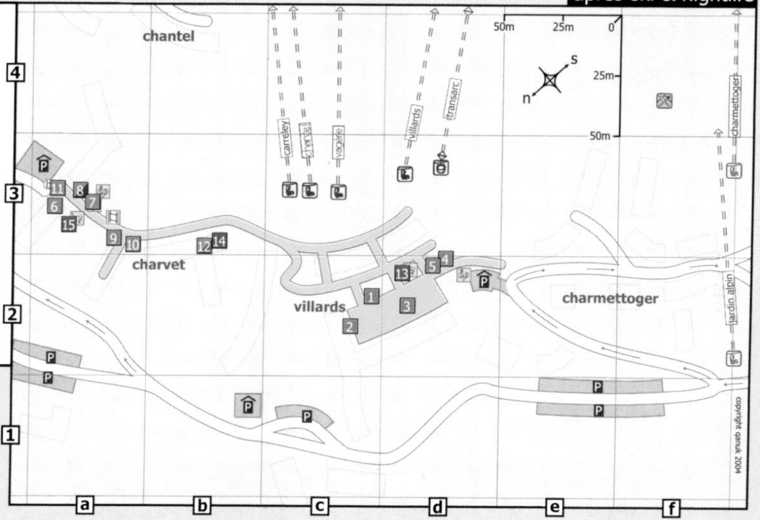

le before

p95
d2

☎ -
🕐 2pm-2am

If the Ambiente isn't quite your thing, you'll find a perfect juxtaposition in the Before. As narrow as the Ambiente is square, the curiously named and shinily decorated bar aims itself largely at English after hours drinkers, and has regular live DJs specializing variously in trance, drum & bass, and occasionally salsa... there is Sky TV to keep the football heads happy, and a cocktail menu for the (footballers') wives. You'll have to move venue when you feel like dancing though, as when it's busy there's barely room enough for your toes to think let alone tap.

96

benji's

p95
c2

☎ -
🕐 12pm-2am

If the resort sometimes feels a little quiet in the evening, it's because everyone is at Benji's. It's not very big, and after 9pm you will literally be lucky to get in the door. No matter when you go you should be prepared to share your company with a large volume of English merrymakers - it is utterly saturated with Island dwellers, and there is no need to know a word of French. In early evening you can get tex-mex food, and though the Mountain Café in Le Charvet has superior offerings for your stomach, if your evening schedule is predominantly concerned with booze this is a required stop on the tour.

hotel du golf

p95
b3

☎ 0479 076500
🕐 3pm-2am

Though strictly speaking a hotel bar, anyone hoping for a jazzy piano bar place is best served here. If you brought a jacket and some smart-ish trousers, this is where you can try them out. The bar is open to non-residents, and is usually busy both pre- and post-dinner.

arc café

p95
a3

☎ -
🕐 8am-1:30am

A very small French hangout, whose best advertisement for foreigners is the Illy coffee. Snowboarders who speak the local lingo will fit right in, but English half-termers whose best effort is '*deux bières*' may not have such a smooth time. Evenings are louder than they are busy - it's such a tiny place that you're unlikely to want to hang around to soak up the atmosphere, and unless you're a seasonnaire you've already stopped reading this review.

jungle café

p95
d2

☎ 0479 071962
🕐 4pm-2am

A long thin bar that is chilled and very French. Music is likely to range through the more funky genres, including reggae and other African-influenced Euro-hoohah. They do a fine Amaretto, and the Frenchness isn't as intimidating as in some spots - the boss is often behind the bar, and will happily engage in nicotine fuelled chit-chat. With a busy crowd it can be fantastic fun, and without one it is a fine place to relax your tired self.

apokalypse

☎ -
🕐 11pm-4am

p95
d2

The 'cool' option in 1800, anyone used to English clubbing will find themselves instantly at home in Apokalypse. It comes with equal doses of pretension and attitude, but also with decent DJs and mainstream club music - mostly R&B, hip-hop and trancey dance. There's comfy seating and a mezzanine level so you can stand and watch the dancefloor, drinks are reassuringly expensive and attendance figures are reliably good. If you can't be bothered with the trip to Café Sol in 1600, this is the best club available.

le fair way

☎ 0479 076500
🕐 10pm-4am

p95
b3

Where Apokalypse is pricey, full of attitude and regularly full to capacity, the Fair Way is cheap, cheerful, and regularly empty. Outside of peak weeks you take pot luck on there being anyone else in the place - but you will find cheesy music and plenty of space on the dancefloor, along with bouncers you can chat to and a very friendly owner who is often behind the bar. And when it is busy, it's every bit as good as the competition - especially post 2am, when people (sometimes) roll in from the other bars.

and the rest

Arc 1800 has a third club - hidden around the corner at the far end of Le Charvet is the recently refurbished **sing island** (t 0479 071967).

97

The central government of the resort ensures that in 1950 no 2 restaurants will offer similar menus, no 2 bars will have similar décor, no 2 rental shops will offer the same range of equipment, and so on. For the time being, of course, there are only 2 rental shops (one for skis and one for boards) and only 2 bars (one of which is really a café)... but the limited range is made up for by 2 things - outstanding quality in what there is, and the Cabriolet link to Arc 2000. And for self-catering families, all you really need is a supermarket.

98

There isn't one - but you can order bread and milk from reception in your apartment building, and you can stock up on supplies on your way through Bourg St. Maurice.

Though the resort is far from finished, the sense of community is already very much in place. The resort is small - which means that everyone that works there knows everyone else that works there, and they always seem to be passing each other on the street and exchanging jolly banter. There is a sort of ambient friendliness to the place, and the resort staff go to every length to instil their cheery enthusiasm into your holiday. From welcome meetings infused with silly French humour to the more practical attractions of free ski-jöering, take-away tartiflette stalls and the occasional vin chaud give away, 1950 has all the ingredients you could possibly want. True, they're not organic

- in fact if there was ever a genetically modified ski resort, this is it - but even so it's very hard to stand in the snow by the outdoor fire in the main street and not be won over by its manufactured charms. You may find yourself saying "It's all a bit faux", but it's unlikely that you'll mean it.

arc 1950

99

copyright qanuk 2004

cabriolet

arc 2000

arc 1600, arc 1800, bourg st. maurice

40m 20m 0
40m 20m

restaurants
1 la casa
2 hemmingway's
bars
3 les belles pintes

<< eating out >>

la casa 🔔🔔🔔

☎ 0479 075648
🕐 9am-11pm
🍴 italian

The first of Arc 1950's restaurants, which interestingly does not serve fondue (one of those on the way). The extensive menu stretches a long way past pizza, and the food is somewhat more expensive than your average Italian - but no matter what you order you are guaranteed good food. Simple continental breakfast is available from 9am, and the main menu from midday to close. The inside is rather yellow, which along with high ceilings makes the whole affair quite light and airy. The ownership has a familial connection with the Privilege bar on Chamonix's Rue des Moulins, and La Casa is a similarly warm, friendly, and relaxing place, whether you're mooching around over a long lunch or easing your way through a pasta dinner.

hemmingway's café 🔔🔔🔔🔔

☎ 0479 041950
🕐 8am-11pm
🍴 international

Doubling as café/bar and up-market restaurant, Hemmingway's is equally good for chilling out with a beer and some peanuts or dining out on carpaccio and veal. There is something for all times of day: the menu includes breakfast and lunch, and the terrace catches the late afternoon sunshine (though it catches the shade all morning). Service is slick and smiling, and the food doesn't disappoint. The restaurant section is adorned with photos of the man himself - and if Hemmingway's philosophy is the same as Hemmingway's (as it were) then they're not far from the mark - the best food in the simplest way.

<< après ski & nightlife >>

les belles pintes

☎ 0479 041950
🕐 10am-2am

A large and rather upmarket feeling pub, split over 3 levels and with a seating capacity of around 150. Depending on where you sit you will either feel like you're in your local boozer, an All Bar One, or someone's living room - and no matter where you are you will be able to see at least 1 plasma screen TV. Décor is very much aimed at the refined English, the bar offers a range of single malt whiskies, live music covers a hotchpotch of styles and is more likely to be jazzy than grungy... but of course the main reason to come is that the Belles Pintes is the only après place in the resort (for now).

snapshot

what intrawest did next

The power behind the throne of Arc 1950 is a little company called Intrawest. Arc 1950 isn't their first venture into making ski resorts - though this is their first bite of the European cherry their teeth have already been well and truly cut on the

other side of the pond. Their enormous CV includes household names like Whistler and Mont Tremblant.

If you have skied in America before, you will know that it is very normal for an entire resort to be run by a single parent company. The commerce is controlled with the intention of providing variety, and though this approach might seem to be anti-competitive, for the risk of paying a Euro or two more you get the chance to actually find what you want rather than traipsing around endless reincarnations of the same middle-of-the-road rental shop or fondue restaurant.

So what's on the menu for Arc 1950? Winter 2004 sees the arrival of a French themed restaurant, a bakery for your morning bread, a cash machine for you to get at your Euros and a nightclub for you to spend them in. On the cards for December 2005 are another restaurant, a newsagent, a chocolate shop, a second Ogier store, a clothing shop and a toy shop. So everyone will be happy.

Front of house operations are taken care by what is called the 'Resort Club'. Their remit is to look after the day-to-day running of the resort, and their input into your holiday ranges from holding welcome meetings to organising free entertainment in the resort every week - like ski-jöering around the nearby slopes and other après-ski fun.

The responsibility for UK marketing is handled by specialist tour operator Erna Low. They have long-standing and close links with Les Arcs and La Plagne, and this ties them very well to provide a link between British skiers and some of the best laid plains in recent skiing history.

Arc 2000's commerce is split between 2 levels, creatively named the Place Haute and the Place Basse. Most of what you want is on the Place Basse, the small stretch of shops that runs along the snow front. Go up in the lift to level 5 and you get to the High Square, where you will find 2000's coolest bar and an irrelevant nightclub. 2000 is so small that you will spend some time wondering if that is really all there is - but the Cabriolet link to Arc 1950 means that if you feel like you're not spending enough money you don't have far to go to lighten your wallet. Much of the English community stays in the chalet complex just below the main resort - there is a second supermarket there, along with a ski shop and 2 bars. Self-caterers be warned - everyone in the 2000 world goes to the small supermarket at about 7pm on Saturday evening, so it may be worth your while stocking up in Bourg St. Maurice before you head up the hill.

102

<< eating out >>

chez eux	£££

🍸 • p103 d1 1

☎ 0479 073436
🕐 11:30am-2:30pm, 7:30-10pm
🍴 international & savoyarde

A step across the threshold of Chez Eux is a step away from Arc 2000's manufactured mass-market feel. The photograph-covered walls and well chosen wood décor give the restaurant a pleasant and sort of sepia feel, and surprisingly the branded chairs don't feel like a step too far. The food is every bit as good as the surroundings: they do hot chocolate that's hot and chocolatey, lunchtime snacks in the usual vein, and an evening menu that though pretty typically Savoyarde in style is more inspiring than your standard range of choices.

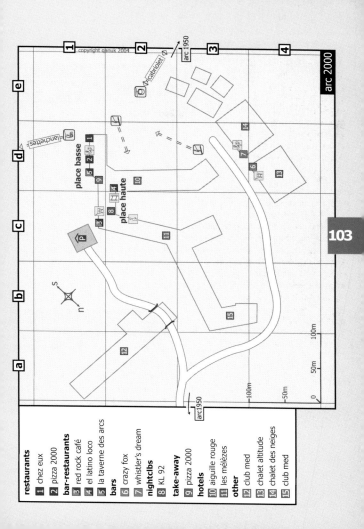

restaurants
1 chez eux
2 pizza 2000

bar-restaurants
3 red rock café
4 el latino loco
5 la taverne des arcs

bars
6 crazy fox
7 whistler's dream

nightclbs
8 KL 92

take-away
9 pizza 2000

hotels
10 aiguille rouge
11 les mélèzes

other
12 club med
13 chalet altitude
14 chalet des neiges
15 club med

arc 2000

arc 1950

cabriolet

landnettes

place basse

place haute

arc1950

P

100m

50m

100m

100m

50m

0

103

la taverne des arcs ££

☎ -
🕐 12-11pm
✕ international & savoyarde

A large and bustling restaurant that is perhaps the best family option in Arc 2000. The menu, while not exhaustively huge, offers entrées ranging from chicken wings to foie gras and main courses from fajitas to fully-fledged braserade with all the trimmings - and it is all available at lunch or supper.

Seemingly busy at all times of day, the Taverne has a separate bar section (with a TV) for your après beer and the whole thing is brought together by a bizarre decorative theme that includes dangling shoes and an assortment of teddy bears sitting on the rafters.

104

and the rest

If neither of these appeals, also available is **pizza 2000** (t 0479 076420), a sweet little pizzeria which offers a limited range of pizza and pasta to eat in or take away.

<< après ski & nightlife >>

red rock café ££

☎ 0479 071058
🕐 12pm-2am
✕ american

Clearly inspired by a more famous Rock Café, this one is American bar/diner through and through. The busiest of 2000's après options, it has something to keep all unrefined tastes happy: pool, video games, TVs, plenty of seating space, and a restaurant which serves - surprisingly - burgers and pizzas, along with pasta and tex-mex choices. The food is inexpensive, the bar is lively, and after 10pm the place turns into more of a night-time facility, adopting the low-lighting and live local DJ approach to proceedings.

el latino loco ££

☎ 0479 077949
🕐 4pm-2am
✕ 'latino'

A very cool bar, about as far from anything to do with skiing as could possibly be wished. Plenty of comfy seating, pool tables with enough space around them to actually play a proper game, a large projection TV that shows films as well as sport and extreme videos... the bar is dark and chilled and offers a range of tequila based drinks and a decent cocktail selection, and the separate restaurant section has a small but appetising (and inexpensive) 'latino' menu.

whistler's dream

p103 d3

- ☎ -
- 🕐 4pm-2am

Whistler's is officially designated an 'English pub'. It doesn't sound very English (though it doesn't sound too French either), it has a VIP room with sofas - not very French. It sells Guinness - enjoyable, and a welcome change to gassy French beer, but again not entirely English. The justification for the description is in the clientele - you are very unlikely to find a French person in Whistler's. It's down in the complex of chalets run by English tour operators, and is one of 2 good reasons not to bother heading up to the main part of the resort.

crazy fox

p103 d4

- ☎ -
- 🕐 4pm-2am

The other reason is the Crazy Fox. Whistler's is cosy and comfy, and the Crazy Fox is, well, a little more crazy. And so more suitable for more outrageous après .But either one is a perfectly good place to spend your evening surrounded by a lot of like minded Englishmen (and Englishwomen), whose make-up is as much seasonnaire as it is holidaymaker.

KL 92

p103 d3

- ☎ -
- 🕐 11pm-4am

Possibly the most outrageous misnomer in the history of clubbing (or speed-skiing), the KL is named after the Kilometre Lancé (➥ events & activities). If you are therefore imagining a nightclub which can match the adrenaline of flying down a snow slope at over 200kph, stop. Arc 2000 doesn't really need a nightclub - and though on some nights it can be a blast, on most is about as exciting as a snowplough on a green run. If you want late night noise, stay in the bar.

105

vallandry & plan-peisey

Actually 2 distinct villages with about 15 minutes worth of walk between them, Vallandry and Plan-Peisey have small-resort welcome in abundance. The restaurants include the superb Armoise, and though there aren't many bars those on offer are crammed with cosy jollity in a way not found so much in the main Les Arcs resorts. Otherwise there is a spattering of typical ski shops and places to buy authentic mountain sausages - though there's not much to fire the imagination, there is at least plenty of space to walk around. And with the Vanoise Express comes more business and hence more investment, so soon that space will be taken up by more bars, more accommodation and more restaurants.

<< eating out >>

le refuge £££

☎ 0479 079659
🕓 4pm-10am
✗ pizza

p107
b3

Le Refuge makes up for its lack of character and unspectacular looks by being the best spot in Vallandry for good cheap pizza - and fondue if you order in advance. It is a small restaurant with no pretensions to grandeur and not much variety on the menu, but it is more relaxed and fun feeling than the Ourson and is ideal for families - though a little cramping for large groups.

le dahu £££

☎ 0479 042096
🕓 4pm-12am
✗ international & savoyarde

p107
a3

The most original restaurant this far round the mountain, the Dahu's newspaper-style menu covers such diversities as bison, kangaroo and ostrich along with the more usual duck and lamb. It's a little way out from Vallandry's main hub, and the neon sign doesn't exactly inspire faith, but it has the friendly welcome so typical to Vallandry along with a superb view across the valley to Montchavin and La Plagne's ski area. Food costs a little more than

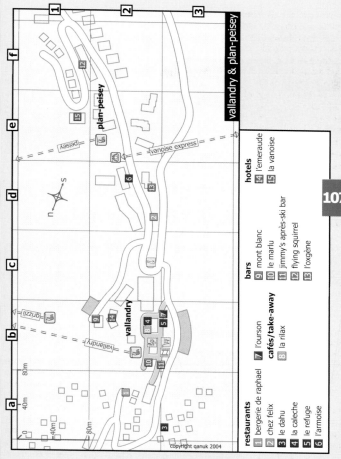

vallandry & plan-peisey

plan-peisey

vallandry

vanoise express

peisey

grizzli

vallandry

n
s

0   40m   80m
40m   80m

copyright qanuk 2004

restaurants

1 bergerie de raphael
2 chez felix
3 le dahu
4 la caleche
5 le refuge
6 l'armoise

7 l'ourson

cafés/take-away

8 la rilax

bars

9 mont blanc
10 le marlu
11 jimmy's après-ski bar
12 flying squirrel
13 l'oxgène

hotels

14 l'emeraude
15 la vanoise

elsewhere, but away from L'Armoise this is the best choice for eating out, and the large open plan layout can cope equally with couples, families and groups.

l'armoise £££

☏ 0479 079424
🕐 6pm-11pm
✕ savoyarde/gourmet

Quite the best of all the restaurants within easy range of Peisey-Vallandry, L'Armoise offers a variety of excellent dishes, along with set-menus that give you 4 or 5 courses for the price of a main in a more up-market resort. These include the *Menu Decouverte* with which you won't know what you're getting until it arrives, the only clues lying in your cutlery. L'Armoise looks deceptively bland from the outside, but aside from this and the slightly low chairs (or high tables) there is not a whiff of a complaint. Food is invariably superb, and though you won't feel like you're in a posh restaurant, you will eat better here than almost anywhere else in Les Arcs.

108

la bergerie du raphael £££

☏ 0479 079495
🕐 12-2:30pm, 7-10pm
✕ traditional savoyarde

Up in the old village on the far side of Vallandry, and close enough to the pistes to qualify it as a mountain restaurant, the Bergerie du Raphael makes a good place to escape the rather humdrum offerings on the main walkway. Food isn't quite in the league of the Dahu, but the chalet surroundings give it a more traditional feel and if your French is any good the owners will be happy to swap a few culinary tales while you peruse the menu.

l'ancolie £££

☏ 0479 079320
🕐 evenings, by reservation only
✕ traditional french

A very special place that is only available to those with cars (or taxi fares), a trip to L'Ancolie is rather like going over to someone's house for dinner. The whole experience is quirkily wonderful, from hand-written menus to food that breathes new life into the word 'homemade'. It only seats 20 at capacity, and you can only eat there by reservation. Dishes are French rather than Savoyarde - you can't get fondue but you can get some fabulous pastries along with a variety of other delicacies. It isn't cheap, but it isn't too expensive either, and for the Francophile L'Ancolie is an absolute must.

l'ourson £££

☎ 0479 079678
🕓 3pm-12pm
✗ savoyarde & pizza

A bar and restaurant that serves up fondues, steaks, pizzas and similarly standard offerings. Prices are a touch above some of the other places on the walkway, but the food is good and the restaurant section is distinct enough from the bar to feel like a separate entity. It's quite a French place, and the bar has something of a local following - but it isn't really an après hangout. Though fine for a quiet beer, you're unlikely to find it a spot for rowdy celebrations, and the atmosphere can't match the 3 main bars.

109

and the rest

Other choices in Vallandry include **la caleche**, a standard steak and fondue place, and **la rilax** (t 0479 042165), a snack and simple dish place by the snow front. A little way up the road towards Plan Peisey is **chez félix** (t 0479 079241).

<< après ski & nightlife >>

jimmy's après-ski bar

☎ 0479 042992
🕐 4pm-2am

p107
b2/3

Jimmy's Après-Ski Bar does what it says on the tin. It's an overtly Dutch entry, which means Eurovision music and dancing to match - both in front of and behind the bar. It is as jolly a place as you could hope to find, and is the most instantly welcoming of the 3 après offerings. Unless it's a slow week in town you're unlikely to find any peace and quiet - though it feels like it might have an upstairs section, it doesn't - the small square room is all there is, but for jumping up and down in your ski gear it's pretty much all you need.

110

le marlu

☎ 0479 042099
🕐 8am-2am

p107
b2

The French side of the bar ménage à trois, the Marlu is small and very... French. It's open for coffee and cigarettes in the morning, snacks at lunch (it's right by the Vallandry lift, so you can sit and watch and wait for the queue to die down), but the main attraction is the evening. They have a live band at least once a week, coordinated with events in the other 2 bars to leave some nights busy and some nights quiet. It strikes a healthily French balance between the consistent population of the Blanc and the sing-song silly dancing of Jimmy's, and though of the 3 options you're least likely to feel at home in here, for live music lovers this is the destination of choice.

le mont blanc

☎ 0479 079234
🕐 9am-12:30am (or 2am)

p107
b2

Known locally just as 'The Blanc', this is the English third of Vallandry's après equation. It is open all day for food and drink, with a full English breakfast to 10:30am, lunch that includes a quick-stop burger shack round the back by the pistes, and an evening meal if you order in advance. But the Blanc is largely about drinking, which takes place in one form or another from early afternoon until early morning. It is attached to the 'hotel' of the same name, which is run by Hucksters and hence provides the bar with plenty of English clientele - add to that its popularity with Vallandry seasonnaires and you have a lively cocktail bar that is the best place in town for your night-time shenanigans.

the flying squirrel

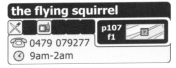

☎ 0479 079277
🕐 9am-2am

p107
f1

Just along from the Vanoise Express, the Flying Squirrel is an English run blend of grill-style food, widescreen live sports, and offbeat evenings that include quiz nights and fancy dress parties. Being in Plan-Peisey it is a bit of a hike to get to if you're staying in Vallandry, but though it's a small place it's worth the trip for a change of scene and for the friendly blend of cultures that is somewhat absent from the bars in the middle of town. Newly refurbished and armed with a pool table and an extended food menu, the Squirrel offers an entirely genuine dose of ski-resort cheer.

and the rest

In between Plan-Peisey and Vallandry is the **oxygène**, whose client base comes from the English tour operator that runs the surrounding chalets. From the road you're likely to assume it's a hoax and give up on finding the bar before you get there - but if you persevere following the signs down the stairs and around the back of the buildings you will eventually reach what is in fact a pleasant and modern chalet bar.

When the lifts are closed because of too little or - more frustratingly - too much snow, there a few things to keep you occupied.

more exercise?

A short hike up from the middle of Arc 1800 is a large **ice rink** (t 0479 074932), cleverly hidden in the trees so as not to be an eyesore. Early evening opening hours (4pm-9pm and until 10pm during school hols) mean you can bundle the kids off while you go and have a pint - or equally go for a romantic spin with your partner before dining out. It all works just the same as your local one back home, with people going round and round and occasionally falling over. Access is free with your lift pass.

112

If you're worried that a week without **squash** (t 0479 074675) will see you slipping down the ladder at work, Arc 1800 has the solution. Open 5pm-9pm access is free with your lift pass, or alternatively you can buy tickets by the half-hour or in groups of 5 or 10 sessions. Especially when it is cloudy you should make sure you reserve, as you are unlikely to be able to simply turn up and play.

For adrenalin rather than actual exercise it is possible these days to experience 'snow-tubing' just across from Arc 2000. Apparently a Canadian invention, snow-tubing is rather like those slides you get at waterparks - you sit on what

is effectively a tire, and slide down the snow until you stop or, more likely, fall off. If this sounds like your thing, contact the Arc 2000 tourist office (t 0479 071378).

To work up a sweat in a slightly different way, the hotel du Golf in 1800 (t 0479 077050) and the hotel La Cachette (t 0479 414343) in 1600 both have **saunas** and **beauty rooms** that non-residents may use for a small fee.

man-made wonders

The top of the Transarc and Plagnettes lifts is home to Les Arcs' most unnecessary tourist attraction - a man-made **ice grotto** (*la grotte de glace*). If you are not content with being able to see nothing but snow-capped peaks for miles and miles, you can spend a few Euros to go into an artificial cave and see some admittedly quite good ice sculptures in an admittedly a suprisingly large grotto. Actually, the cave is quite the winter tardis, and though it is tempting to say that it's all a bit of a waste when there's so much to do outside, you may find yourself impressed with the workmanship. Perhaps more importantly, young children will be fascinated - and a lot less likely to fall over and hurt themselves than when they're on the piste.

take to the skies

Jumping off mountains with a parachute is often quite a scary prospect, but if you believe you can fly, by **parapenting** you will experience the ski area from a very unusual, breathtaking and surprisingly peaceful perspective. Jumps are obviously taken in tandem with an instructor, and can start from any of 4 spots around the area. Darentesia is a specialist parapenting school, or the ESF or Arc Adventures offer tandem jumps (➡ lessons & guiding for contact details).

culture vulture

With the exception of Arc 1950, all of the resorts have a **cinema** (1600 t 0479 077934, 1800 t 0479 074137, 2000 t 0479 073581, Vallandry t 0479 079669). They tend to be quite busy places - much as with the ice rink, packing the kids off to watch a film is a great way to work yourself some well-earned downtime while making it look like you're being generous. All show VO films (*Version Originale*) on a regular basis. Listings are posted on the boards around the respective resorts.

head for the valleys

If the weather's bad or you need a day away, **bourg st. maurice** is only 7 minutes by Funicular from Arc 1600. There you will find museums, a swimming pool, and all the trappings of a decent-sized town - including coffee shops, clothes shops, book shops, gift shops, food shops, outdoor shops... in short, some shops. Also, a big supermarket, and plenty of space. If your stomach hasn't had enough fondue you can visit the Diary Cooperative at the Rond Point de la Gare to see how the Savoie cheeses are made (t 0479 070828, Mondays-Fridays 9:30am-11:30am). The claustrophobic will be happy to hear that in addition to all the shops, there are often no clouds on the valley floor even when the resorts are in a white-out.

children

Though not as children-friendly as La Plagne - perhaps an unfair comparison as La Plagne is *the* family resort - it is one of France's P'tit Montagnards resorts, a status only awarded to spots with more than enough going on to keep the little ones happy.

tour operators

Many operators have discounted or free child places in their chalets and some also include free ski and boot hire, lift passes or ski lessons for children. In addition, a few operators run childcare programmes. The forerunner is probably **esprit** - a leading light in family ski holidays they are old-hands at it having run a childcare programme for over 20 years. In Arc 2000 and Peisey-Vallandry they offer services from a nursery for children aged 4 months-3 years (6 full days 8:30am-5pm) to a range of ski classes for children aged 3-12 years. An even greater attraction for some parents will be the evening classes run for 6-12 year olds. The **family ski company** is a small company based in Les Coches that offers a crèche for 0-4 year olds (9am-4:30pm, Sundays-Fridays) and a post-ski school club for 4-11 year olds. Larger operators such as **crystal** and **thomson** also offer childcare programmes though these differ according to which Les Arc resort you are staying in. **club med** has 2 hotels in Les Arcs - the one in 2000 is a 'family village'. Skiing, tuition and childcare for children over 4 years are included in the

price of their holidays. Not an operator as such, **snowkidz private nannies** (t 01962 881188, i snowkidz.com) is a UK company which places nannies in certain ski resorts around the Alps, of which Les Arcs is one. All nannies are fully qualified and are available Sundays-Friday 9am-5pm. They will come to your accommodation to look after your child - one nanny can look after 2 children aged under 2 years and 3 children over 3 years.

in-resort

1600's day **nursery** (*garderie*) is based in the hotel Cachette (t 0479 077050) 7 days a week (8:30am-13:30pm, 2pm-6pm) and takes children aged 4 months-11years. In 1800, Le Pomme de Pin (t 0479 042431, i miniclub.ski-lesarcs.com) takes 1-6 year olds, 7 days a week (8:45am-12pm, 2pm-5:30pm). In 2000 the nursery is called Les Marmottons (t 0479 076425), takes children aged 2-6 years and is open

undays-Fridays (8:30am-12pm,
:30pm-7pm).

or older children who ski all of Les
rcs' branches of the ESF have a
arderie (**kindergarten**) and a Club
iou Piou - a skiing-dedicated club for
hildren aged 3 and above which is run
n a protected zone and has ski lifts
uitable for children. Either the local
ourist office or the local ESF office will
e able to give you details. Arc
Adventures in 1800 take children aged 4
nd above and Spirit in 1950 also runs
group lessons for children. Children
must wear a helmet to join a group
esson. All the ski rental shops have
helmets for hire - though make sure
you get one that fits well. Many a
antrum has been thrown because of an
ll-fitting helmet.

Children aged 5 and under ski for free
in Les Arcs and the Paradiski area and 1
child under 7 is entitled to a free lift
pass for every paying parent (for a
period of the same length).

Children can join in most of the
activities on offer - from ice-skating to
snowtubing. Throughout the season the
tourist offices organise various events
for children - from Mardi Gras fancy
dress parties to downhill slaloms.
Contact the tourist office in your resort
for events on during your stay.

115

before you go

Before you decide what kind of job you want you need to decide what kind of season you want - a job as a rep will be better paid but you have more responsibility, while a job as a chalet host means fixed hours, but once you know the routine, more time to make the most of resort life. Most of the UK ski companies recruit seasonal workers - interviewing normally starts in May, though there may still be vacancies as late as December. Either contact the companies directly (not forgetting smaller or overseas based ones)or go through a recruitment website such **natives** (i natives.co.uk) who has a comprehensive database of available jobs as well as a lot of useful information on everything about "doing a season". It's a competitive market for jobs and while it is not essential, speaking reasonable French will help. If you haven't got a job by October, it's worth going to the Ski Show at Olympia - some tour operators have a stall there as does Natives. If you haven't got a job by the start of the season, it can still be worth heading out to the resort (if you can support yourself for a bit). Some of the less glamorous jobs may still be available and you will also get known - so when there is the inevitable fall-out of recruits due to unsuitability, New Year flu and mid-season blues, you can step into the role. Jobs constantly become available throughout the season - the ski market is very transient.

116

Once employed most companies organise your travel to and from the resort, accommodation, lift pass and equipment rental. Most seasonnaire jobs come with a shared room as part of the 'incentives' package. This is not true of many bar jobs - but your boss may well be able to put you in touch with someone who will help you to find somewhere to stay. If accommodation doesn't come with your job - or if you aren't planning on having a job - you would be well advised to find some digs before you head out. There are a handful of companies that offer longer term rentals, generally offering shared accommodation. Single or double apartments are a little harder to come by, and accordingly can be pretty pricey. Planet SubZero is a good place to start (i planetsubzero.com) - they are based in Vallandry and have chalet accommodation there, along with rooms in Arc 2000.

The likelihood is that your job will only provide you with a lift pass for Les Arcs. You can buy an extension to your season pass to cover all of Paradiski, though as the best skiing in Paradiski is above Les Arcs' resorts, a trip over to La Plagne would only be for a change of scenery or to have a go at the infamous off-piste run off the north face of the Bellecôte.

once you're there

Just as the different resorts make for different holidays, so they make for very different seasons. The biggest seasonnaire community is in 1800 - though there is normally not much interplay between the French and English sides of the scene. The bastions of English culture are Benji's and the Saloon - particularly in Benji's you will almost never find a Frenchman or hear a word of the local lingo. Arc 2000 also has a sizeable contingent thanks to the 'chalets' just under the resort. The nightlife is pretty lively, though the KL92 is more often than not overlooked for being too far up the hill when you've got Whistler's and the Fox rather closer to your bed. Vallandry, though a little around the corner and not an obvious choice, is actually perhaps a better spot to work a season. The community has fewer than 100 seasonnaires, and as a result everybody gets to know everybody else fairly quickly.

internet is close to impossible. None of the resorts have a internet café - though there is a terminal in Arc 2000's Red Rock café - or indeed anything resembling one. The tourist offices have terminals and will let you hook-up a laptop to your connection, should one be part of your packing. Aside from that some of the hotels have internet points - such as La Cachette in 1600 or Le Thuria in 1800 -which operate either with telecom internet cards (which you will be able to buy from the reception of the relevant hotel) or with whatever system the hotel has set up. You won't find broadband anywhere, and many of

the internet terminals are very old and therefore rather decrepit. Though if all you need is somewhere to chek your email once a week you ought to be able to do that.

All the resorts have **laundry** facilities, **mini-supermarkets** and **pharmacies**, so most of your basic needs are covered. For more substantial requirements you will need transport of some kind - Bourg St. Maurice is very close and if you can get to 1600 (or live there anyway) it's just under 8 minutes away by funicular.

Calls home are expensive from an English **mobile**, so it could be worth investing in a French SIM card - generally about £30 (of which £15 is credit) and calls made within and out of France will be cheaper and you won't pay to receive calls from the UK. Check that your phone is 'unlocked' (so you can insert a foreign SIM card - available in Bourg) before you leave the UK. You then pay as you go as you would in the UK. Top up cards are available from the various tabacs and bookshops around town.

For anything you need after you arrive there is a *maison des saisonniers* in Arc 1800 (t 0479 010135). They know the ins and outs of season life and should be able to point you in the right direction whatever your problem may be.

117

the a-z

tour operators

A number of English based tour operators offer holidays to Les Arcs. Though many of them offer a variety of skiing holidays they are categorised according to their main strength.

mainstream
airtours t 0870 238 7777, i mytravel.com
club med t 0700 2582932, i clubmed.co.uk
crystal t 0870 405 5047, i crystalski.co.uk
equity travel t 01273 886 879,
i equity.co.uk
first choice t 0870 754 3477, i fcski.co.uk
french life ski t 0870 197 6692,
i frenchlifeski.co.uk
inghams t 020 8780 4433, i inghams.co.uk
leisure direction t 020 8324 4042,
i leisuredirection.co.uk
neilson t 0870 333 3356,
i neilson.co.uk
thomson t 0870 606 1470,
i thomson-ski.co.uk

ski-specific
directski.com t 0800 587 0945,
i directski.com
handmade holidays t 01285 648 518,
i handmade-holidays.co.uk
on the piste travel t 01625 503 111,
i onthepiste.co.uk
rocketski.com t 01273 262626,
i rocketski.com
ski activity t 01738 840 888,
i skiactivity.co.uk
ski beat t 01243 780 405, i skibeat.co.uk
ski club of great britain t 020 8410 2022, i skiclub.co.uk
ski esprit t 01252 618300, i ski-esprit.co.uk

ski independence t 0870 600 1462,
i ski-independence.co.uk
ski olympic t 01302 328 820,
i skiolympic.co.uk
total ski t 08701 633 633, i skitotal.com
ski world t 08702 416723,
i skiworld.ltd.uk

les arcs specific
family ski holidays t 01684 540333/541444, i familyski.co.uk
ski adventures t 0033 321 048221,
i skiadventures.co.uk
ski hiver t 02392 428586, i skihiver.co.uk

self-catering & budget
ams t 01743 340623, i amsrentals.com
interhome t 020 8891 1294,
i interhome.co.uk
ski amis t 0207 692 0850, i skiamis.com
ski france4less t 01724 290660,
i french-freedom.co.uk

self-drive
drive alive t 0114 292 2971, i drive-alive.com
erna low t 0207 584 2841,
i ernalow.co.uk
eurotunnel motoring holidays t 0870 333 2001, i eurotunnel.com

tailor-made & weekends
made to measure holidays t 0124 353 3333, i madetomeasureholidays.com

If you run a ski company that offers holidays to Les Arcs but are not listed here, let us know and we'll include you in the next edition of this guide.

directory

listings

All 04 or 06 numbers need the French international prefix (0033) if dialled from the UK. 08 numbers can only be dialled within France.

Almost anything you could want is available from Bourg St. Maurice - so though the resorts may be a little under equipped you are never more than an hour away from what you need.

transport

air

bmibaby t 0870 264 2229,
i bmibaby.com
british airways t 0870 850 9850,
i ba.com
easyjet t 0870 600 0000,
i easyjet.co.uk
ryanair i ryanair
swiss t 0845 601 0956, i swiss.com
chambéry t 0479 544966, i aeroport-chambery.com
geneva t 0041 22 717 7111,
i gva.ch
grenoble t 0476 654848,
i grenoble.aeroport.fr
lyon t 0826 800826, i lyon.aeroport.fr
st. etienne t 0477 557171, i saint-etienne.aeroport.fr

car hire

alamo i alamo.com
avis i avis.com
(Moûtiers) t 0479 240793
easycar t 0906 333 3333
i easycar.com
europcar i europcar.com
(Bourg St. Maurice) t 0479 040420
hertz t 0870 844 8844 i hertz.co.uk
(Moûtiers) t 0479 240775

cross-channel

eurotunnel t 0870 535 3535,
i eurotunnel.com
norfolkline t 01304 218400,
i norfolkline.com
speedferries t 01304 203000
i speedferries.com

directory

coach travel
eurolines t 08705 143219,
i nationalexpress.com

driving
general - carry a valid driver's licence,
proof of ownership, your insurance
certificate and an emergency triangle.
petrol - there are petrol stations in
Bourg St. Maurice, but none on the
mountain.
signs & rules - motorways in France
have blue signs. Most operate a *péage*
(toll) system. You must wear a seatbelt
in the front and back of a car. Children
under 12 must sit in the back and
babies and young children must be
placed in special baby/young child
seats.
speed limits - in built-up areas the
speed limit is 50km/h (unless indicated).
The limit is 90km/h on all other roads,
110km/h on toll-free motorways and
130km/h on toll motorways. Foreign
drivers are given spot fines for
speeding.
traffic info - recorded traffic
information 0826 022022.

international train
raileurope t 0870 584 8848
i raileurope.co.uk
eurostar t 0870 518 6186
i eurostar.com
TGV i tgv.com

local train
bourg-1600 funicular t 0479 042400,
i ski-lesarcs.com

SNCF t 0892 353535
i ter-sncf.com/rhone-alpes

private bus
alp line t 0677 865282, i alp-line.com
alpine cab i alpinecab.com.
ATS t 0709 209 7392 i a-t-s.net
mountain transfers t 07889 942786,
i mountaintransfers.com

public bus
cars martin t 0479 070449, i autocars-
martin.com (with branches in the tourist
office in 1600 and 1800).
satobus t 0472 359496
transavoie t 0479 242158, i transavoie-
moutiers.com

directory

health & safety

accidents

If you have an accident on the slopes, you will be taken to the nearest doctor unless you specify a particular one. To confirm you can pay for treatment you will need a credit card and your insurance details. At some point, contact your insurance company to check whether they want to arrange your transport home - and ask your doctor for a medical certificate confirming you are fit to travel. If you see an accident on the slopes, tell the nearest rescue centre, usually found at the top or bottom of lifts.

doctors

1600 t 0479 077857, 1800 t 0479 074060, 2000 t 0479 073001 and Plan-Peisey t 0479 079492 (surgery opening times 9am-12pm, 2pm-7pm). The nearest hospital is in Bourg.

emergency numbers

emergencies t 18 (from a land line), t 112 (from a mobile)
piste security t 0479 070110
bloodwagon t 0479 078566
police t 17
emergency medical care (SAMU) t 15
police municipale t 0479 076202 (1800), t 0479 076422 (2000)
gendarmerie t 0479 074143 (1600)

health

An E111 form (available from any UK post office) entitles you to treatment under the French health system. While you have to pay for your treatment when you receive it, you can then get a refund for up to 70% of medical expenses - as long as you keep all your receipts.

insurance

It is essential to have personal insurance covering wintersports and the cost of any ambulances, helicopter rescue and emergency repatriation - all these services are very expensive. Insurance policies differ greatly - some exclude off-piste skiing or cover it only if you are with a guide, so you need to check the terms and conditions carefully.

pharmacies

1600 t 0479 077734, 1800 t 0479 074054 and plan-peisey t 0479 079492

physiotherapists

1600 t 0479 041389, 1800 t 0479 074142/0479 073771/0479 074999 and 2000 t 0479 041821

safety on the mountain

avalanche danger - the risk of avalanche is graded from 1 to 5.
1 & 2. (yellow) low risk.
3 & 4. (checked yellow and black) moderate risk, caution advised when skiing off-piste
5. (black) high risk, off-piste skiing strongly discouraged.
The risk is displayed on a flag at the main lift stations, but if you are in any doubt about where it is safe to ski, ask

123

directory

the advice of the lift operators.

food & drink - a skiing holiday is not the time to start a diet. Your body expends energy keeping warm and exercising so it's a good idea to eat a decent breakfast, and carry some chocolate or sweets with you.
The body dehydrates more quickly at altitude and whilst exercising. You need to drink a lot (of water) each day to replace the moisture you lose.

rules of conduct - the International Ski Federation publishes conduct rules for all skiers and boarders:

1. respect - do not endanger or prejudice others.
2. control - ski in control, adapting speed and manner to ability, the conditions and the traffic.
3. choice of route - the uphill skier must choose his route so he does not endanger skiers ahead.
4. overtaking - allowed above or below, right or left, but leave enough room for the overtaken skier.
5. entering & starting a run - look up and down the piste when doing so.
6. stopping on the piste - avoid stopping in narrow places or where visibility is restricted.
7. climbing - keep to the side of the piste when climbing up or down.
8. signs & markings - respect these.
9. assistance - every skier must assist at accidents.
10. identification - all involved in an accident (including witnesses) must exchange details.

snow and avalanche information
t 0892 681020

weather
Get daily updates on t 0892 680273 (French) or i meteo.fr or listen to Radio Les Arcs (93.4FM)

what to wear
Several, thin layers are better than one thick piece. Avoid cotton, which keeps moisture next to the body, so cooling it down. A windproof and waterproof material (such as Goretex) is best for outer layers. A hat is essential to keep you warm and protect the scalp from sunburn as are gloves to keep hands warm. Sunglasses or goggles are essential. Wrap-arounds are a good choice and lenses should be shatter-proof and give 100% protection from UVA and UVB rays. Poor eye protection can lead to snowblindness, which makes the eyes water and feel painful and gritty. Treat by resting eyes in a darkened room, and applying cold compresses. You should wear UVA and UVB sun protection with a high factor (SPF) at all times, even if overcast and cloudy. The sun is more intense at higher altitude, so you should re-apply regularly (particularly after falling or sweating). Don't forget to cover your ear lobes and the underside of the nose.

directory

resort survival

banks & atms
With the exception of 1950 (which will have 1 in time for winter 2005-6), all the resorts have a cashpoint. 1800 has 3 banks: Banque de Savoie (t 0479 076526), Banque Populaire (t 0820 337923) and Crédit Agricole (t 0479 074045). They all have cashpoints, and there is a fourth at the post office.

church services
Weekly religious services are held at La Coupole (the tourist office) building in Arc 1600 (t 0479 077070).

internet/email
Internet access is very limited
➜ seasonnaires for more details.

laundry & dry cleaning
There is an automated laundry service by the photo shop in 1600 (at the end of the commercial walkway). 1800 has 2, 1 in Les Villards and 1 at the outer end of Le Charvet (which also has a dry-cleaning service). In 2000 there is 1 on the Place Haute, next to Twinner. 1950 has no DIY laundry facilities but wherever you are staying will be able to organise it for you. In Vallandry there is a *laverie* on the commercial walkway.

maps
The tourist office has maps of the resorts, but they aren't great and don't show much more than where the accommodation is. The topography map

covering the Paradiski area at 1:25,000 is IGN 3532ET.

newspapers
You will rarely see an English paper - you can order them from the newsagents (*presse*) but as a rule they are not stocked. As with anything, in 1950 the best course of action is to ask at the reception of your accommodation.

parking
There is plenty of parking space around all the resorts. 1600 and 1800 have both open air and covered parking - the latter is closer to the resorts and more expensive to use. As you drive up towards 1950 you pass a barrier where you collect a ticket - if you stay in 2000 you will be charged as you leave. 1950 has its own underground car park for which you pay on a per-day basis - you still need the original ticket from the barrier, but you will not be charged as you leave. There is a park-and-ride alternative to this system - you can leave your car in the car park before the barrier, by the Charmettoger chairlift and the Au Pré Gourmand restaurant. It's much cheaper to stay here, and there is a free shuttle up to Arc 2000. Vallandry and Plan-Peisey are much more relaxed and much less organised about parking. Spaces (all outdoor) are governed by a pay-and-display system.

post
There are post offices in 1600 (t 0479 074211), 1800 (t 0479 074178) and

directory

2000 (t 0479 073011). The nearest post office to Peisey-Vallandry is down in Landry.

radio stations
Radio Les Arcs (Europe 2) 93.4FM with English news at 9am and 6pm
Fun Radio 94.9FM
NRJ 100.4FM

shopping
Most shops open every day (except public holidays) 8:30am-12:30pm and 2:30pm-7pm.
supermarkets - with the exception of 1950, every resort has a small supermarket, either a Spar or a Sherpa. They are generally well enough supplied but are all a touch overpriced. If you are driving to resort your best bet is to stock up in Bourg St. Maurice before heading up the hill - there is a Lidl for cheap wine and a huge Super-U for food.
local produce - there are stores in 1800 and Vallandry where you can buy authentic Savoyarde produce (at a slightly inflated price).
clothes - the larger ski shops stock most outdoor brands and accessories.

taxis
a aéro burgod t 0686 242383
a arcs taxis t 0479 074795
ags taxis t 0479 401100
station taxis t 0479 070394
taxis drouet t 0615 551551
taxi benoit (Peisey-Vallandry) t 0611 429957

tourist offices
i lesarcs.com
1600 t 0479 077070
(Mondays-Fridays 10am-12pm, 4pm-6:30pm, Saturdays 9am-12pm, 2pm-7pm, Sundays 10am-12pm, 4pm-7pm)
1800 t 0479 076111
(Mondays-Fridays 9am-12pm, 3:30pm-7pm, Saturdays 8:30am-7pm, Sundays 9am-12pm, 3pm-7pm)
1950 (resort club) t 0479 043020/041900, i arc1950.com
(Saturdays 9am-12:30pm, 2:30pm-7pm, Sundays 9am-12:30pm, 4pm-6:30pm)
2000 t 0479 071378
(Mondays-Thursdays 9am-12pm, 3:45pm-6:45pm, Fridays 9am-12pm, 4pm-6:45pm, Saturdays 8:30am-7:30pm, Sundays 9am-12pm, 2:45pm-6:45pm)
vallandry t 0479 079428
bourg. st maurice t 0479 070492
(Mondays-Fridays 9am-12pm, 2pm-7pm, Saturdays 9am-12:30pm, 2pm-7pm and Sundays 9am-12pm, 3pm-6pm)

country survival

customs

As France is part of the EU, there are few restrictions on what UK visitors can take out for personal use.

electricity

220 volts/50hz ac. Appliances use a two-pin plug - adaptors are readily available.

language

English is widely spoken, though an attempt at French is widely appreciated.

money

The currency is the Euro (€). €1 is equivalent to 100 centimes. Notes come in anything from €10 to €500. You can exchange money in all the banks during the week, and also at the airports and in major train stations. In 2004, the average exchange rate for UK£1 = (approx) €1.6

public holidays

December   6 - St Nicholas Day
             25 - Christmas Day
             26 - St Stephen's day
January   1 - New Year's Day
March/April Good Friday, Easter Sunday & Monday

telephone

Public phones boxes are few and far between, and accept coins or phonecards, which can be bought from the post office, tabacs, and train and petrol stations. All local and calls within Europe are cheaper 7pm-8am during the week and all day at the weekend. The international dialling code for France is 0033; the free international operator t 12; the international directory information t 1159; and national directory information t 111. There are 3 mobile phone networks: Bouyges Telecom, France telecom/Orange and SFR.

time

France is always 1 hour ahead of England.

tipping

All food bills include a service charge, though it is common to make an addition for drinks or for noticeably good service.

water

Tap water is drinkable, except where there is an eau non potable sign.

glossary

a

arête - a sharp ridge.

avalanche - a rapid slide of snow down a slope.

avalanche transceiver - a device used when skiing off-piste, which can both emit and track a high frequency signal to allow skiers lost in an avalanche or a crevasse to be found.

b

BASI - British Association of Snowsport Instructors.

binding - attaches boot to ski.

black run/piste - difficult, generally steeper than a red piste.

blood wagon - a stretcher on runners used by ski patrollers to carry injured skiers off the mountain.

blue run/piste - easy, generally wide with a gentle slope.

bubble ➜ 'gondola'.

button (or Poma) lift - for 1 person. Skis and boards run along the ground, whilst you sit on a small 'button' shaped seat.

c

cable car - a large box-shaped lift, running on a thick cable over pylons high above the ground, which carry up to 250 people per car.

carving - a recently developed turning technique used by skiers and boarders to make big, sweeping turns across the piste.

carving skis - shorter and fatter than traditional skis, used for carving turns.

chairlift - like a small and uncomfortable sofa, which scoops you and your skis off the ground and carries you up the mountain. Once on, a protective bar with a rest for your skis holds you in place. Can carry 2-6 people.

couloir - a 'corridor' between 2 ridges, normally steep and narrow.

crampons - spiked fittings attached to outdoor or ski boots to climb mountains or walk on ice.

d

draglift or (T-bar) - for 2 people. Skis and boards run on the ground, whilst you lean against a small bar.

drop-off - a sharp increase in gradient.

e

edge - the metal ridge on the border of each side of the ski.

f

FIS - Federation Internationale du Ski.

flat light - lack of contrast caused by shadow or cloud, making it very difficult to judge depth and distance.

freeriding, freeskiing - off-piste skiing.

freestyle - skiing involving jumps.

g

glacier - a slow-moving ice mass formed thousands of years ago and fed each year by fresh snow.

gondola (or bubble) - an enclosed lift, often with seats.

h

heliskiing - off-piste skiing on routes only accessible by helicopter.

high season - weeks when the resort is (generally) at full capacity.

i

itinerary route (yellow) - not groomed, maintained or patrolled.

glossary

Generally more difficult, at least in part, than a black piste. Can be skied without a guide.

k

kicker - jump.

l

lambchop drag ➙ 'rope tow'.

ledgy - off-piste conditions in which there are many short, sharp drop-offs.

low season - beginning and end of the season and the least popular weeks in mid-January.

m

mid season - reasonably popular weeks in which the resort is busy but not full.

mogul - a bump, small or large, on or off piste. A large mogulled area is called a mogul field.

o

off-piste - the area away from marked, prepared and patrolled pistes.

p

parallel turn - skis turn in parallel.

piste - a ski run marked, groomed and patrolled, and graded in terms of difficulty (blue, red or black).

piste basher - a bulldozer designed to groom pistes by smoothing snow.

pisteur - a ski piste patroller.

Poma ➙ 'button lift'.

powder - fresh, unbashed or untracked snow.

r

raquettes ➙ 'snowshoes'.

red run/piste - intermediate, normally steeper than a blue piste, although a flatish piste may be a red because it is narrow, has a steep drop-off or because snow conditions are worse than on other pistes.

rope tow (or lambchop drag) - a constantly moving loop of rope with small handles to grab onto to take you up a slope.

s

schuss - a straight slope down which you can ski very fast.

seasonnaire - an individual who lives (and usually works) in a ski resort for the season.

skis - technology has changed in the last 10 years. New skis are now shorter and wider. When renting, you will be given a pair approx. 5-10cms shorter than your height.

ski patrol - a team of piste patrollers

skins - artificial fur attached to ski base, for ski touring.

snow-chains - chains attached to car tyres so that it can be driven (cautiously) over snow or ice.

snowshoes - footwear resembling tennis rackets which attach to shoes, for walking on soft snow.

spring snow - granular, heavy snow conditions common in late season (when daytime temperatures rise causing snow to thaw and re-freeze).

steeps - a slope with a very steep gradient.

t

T-bar ➙ 'draglift'.

w

white-out - complete lack of visibility caused by enveloping cloud cover.

index

index

131

further information

also available the snowmole guides to...

france
chamonix mont-blanc
courchevel les 3 vallées
la plagne paradiski
méribel les 3 vallées
val d'isère espace kily
switzerland
verbier val de bagnes
zermatt matterhorn

coming soon the snowmole guides to...

st. anton arlberg
tignes espace killy
ski weekends

& also the underground network

accuracy & updates

We have tried our best to ensure that all the information included is accurate at the date of publication. However, because places change - improve, get worse, or even close - you may find things different when you get there. Also, everybody's experience is different and you may not agree with our opinion. You can help us, in 2 ways: by letting us know of any changes you notice and by telling us what you think - good or bad - about what we've written. If you have any comments, ideas or suggestions, please write to us at: snowmole, 45 Mysore Road, London, SW11 5RY or send an email to comments@snowmole.com

snowmole.com

Our website is intended as a compliment to our guides. Constantly evolving and frequently updated with news, you will find links to other wintersport related websites, information on our stockists and offers and the latest news about future editions and new titles. We also use our website to let you know of any major changes that occur after we publish the guides.

If you would like to receive news and updates about our books by email, please register your details at www.snowmole.com

order form

The snowmole guides are available from all major bookshops, wintersports retailers or direct from Qanuk Publishing & Design Ltd. To experience the Alps without leaving home have your next snowmole guide delivered to your door. To order send an email to sales@snowmole.com or fill in the form below and send it to us at Qanuk Publishing & Design Ltd, 45 Mysore Road, London, SW11 5RY

the snowmole guide to:	ISBN	quantity
chamonix mont blanc	0-9545739-3-5	-------------------------
courchevel les 3 vallées	0-9545739-5-1	-------------------------
la plagne paradiski	0-9545739-8-6	-------------------------
les arcs paradiski	0-9545739-7-8	-------------------------
méribel les 3 vallées	0-9545739-4-3	-------------------------
val d'isère espace killy	0-9545739-9-4	-------------------------
verbier val de bagnes	0-9545739-2-7	-------------------------
zermatt matterhorn	0-9545739-6-X	-------------------------

total: -------------------------
(£6.99 each, postage & packaging free)

I enclose a cheque for £
(made payable to Qanuk Publishing & Design Ltd)

name --
address ---
postcode --
tel ---
email address ---
(please use block capitals)

Delivery will normally be within 14 working days. The availability and published prices quoted are correct at the time of going to press but are subject to alteration without prior notice. Please note that this service is only available in the UK.

Qanuk would like to keep you updated on new titles in the snowmole range or special offers. If you do not wish to receive such information please tick here ☐
Qanuk has a number of partners in the ski industry, and we may from time to time share your details with those partners if we think it might be of interest to you. If you do not wish us to share your details please tick here ☐

about you

Your comments, opinions and recommendations are very important to us. To help us improve the snowmole guides, please take a few minutes to complete this short questionnaire. Once completed please send it to us at Qanuk Publishing & Design Ltd.

name (Mr/Mrs/Ms) --
address ---
postcode --
email address ---
age ---
occupation --

1. about your ski holiday (circle as appropriate)
how many days do you ski each year?
weekend/1 week/2 weeks/1 month/more
when do you book?
last-minute/1 month before/1-3 months before/3-6 months before/6+ months before
how do you book your holiday?
travel agent/mainstream tour operator/ski-specific tour operator/diy

2. about the snowmole guide
which title did you buy? --
where and when did you buy it? --
have you bought any other snowmole guides? ----------------------------
if so, which one(s) ---
how would you rate each section out of 5 (1 = useless, 5 = very useful)
getting started ---
the skiing --
the resort --
the directory ---
the maps ---
what in particular made you buy this guide? ----------------------------
----
do you have any general comments or suggestions? ---------------------
----
did you buy any other guides for your holiday? -------------------------
if yes, which one? --
Qanuk Publishing & Design Ltd may use information about you to provide you with details of other products and services, by telephone, email or in writing. If you do not wish to receive such details please tick here ☐

about us

snowmole / snōmōl / n. & v. **1** a spy operating within alpine territory (esp. ski resorts) for the purpose of gathering local knowledge. **2** (in full **snowmole guide**) the guidebook containing information so gathered. v. research or compile or process intelligence on an alpine resort or surrounding mountainous area.

the authors

Isobel Rostron and Michael Kayson are snowsport enthusiasts who met while taking time out from real life to indulge their passion - Isobel to get it out of her system and Michael to ingrain it further. Michael's approach having won, they decided that a return to real life was overrated and came up with a cunning plan to make their passion their work. The result was snowmole.

acknowledgements & credits

None of this would have been possible without the help and support of many people:
Joanna Yellowlees-Bound & Fiona Crook (Erna Low), Steph Lightfoot, Judge, Will Nicholson, Tracker, Louise Povah, Sue Windsor, Albin, Andrew Lilley, and Angela Horne, Julian Horne, Henry & Katie Fyson, Tom Fyson, Maisie, Peter & Christine Rostron for their ongoing support.

The publishers would also like to thank the following for their kind permission to reproduce their photographs.
front cover: Office de Tourisme de Les Arcs
back cover: Office de Tourisme de Courchevel 1850 & Office de Tourisme de La Plagne
inside: pages 10, 14 (Aiguille Rouge), 15, 22, 25, 29, 30, 31, 49, 52, 54, 84, 88, 76, 112, 113, 114, & 115 - Office de Tourisme de Les Arcs, title page & pages 14 (Vanoise Express) & 75 Selalp, pages 98 & 101- Intrawest, pages 59, 62, 65, 71, 73, 74 & 106 Office de Tourisme de La Plagne and page 77 Nigel Tench.
The remaining photographs are held in the publisher's own photo library and were taken by Isobel Rostron.

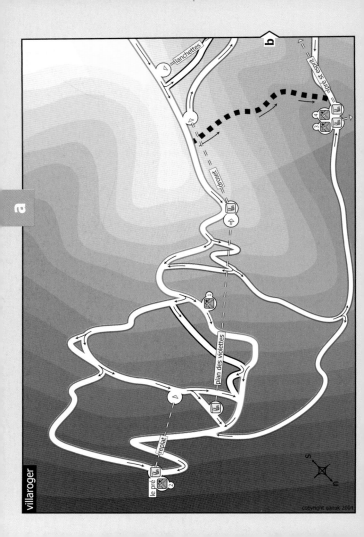

villaroger

	lift	⏱	pistes			queues	moguls I	moguls II	moguls III	off-piste I	off-piste II	off-piste III
replat	3	5m15	■			🚶						
plan des violettes	3	12m00	■	■	■						●	
droset	4	7m30	■	■					●		●	●
pré st esprit	3	13m50	■							●		

i plan des violettes — the lift is in shade from midday onwards, and can be very cold

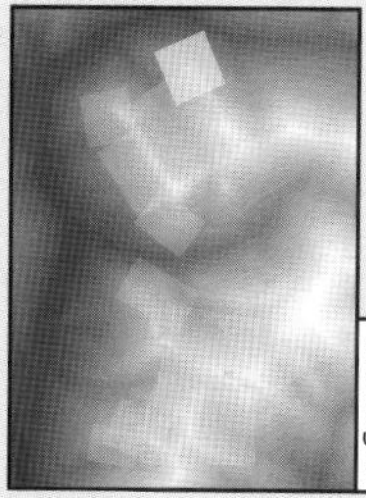

villaroger

1	le solliet
2	la ferme
3	au pré gourmand
4	belliou la fumée

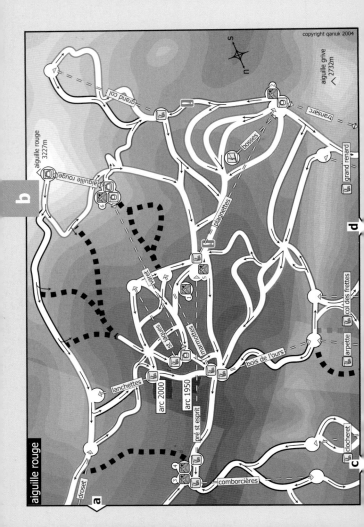

aiguille rouge

copyright qanuk 2004

aiguille grive 2732m

transarc

grand renard

col des frettes

arpette

aiguille rouge 3227m

aiguille rouge

grand col

bosses

plagnettes

varet

st jacques

marmottes

bois de l'ours

lanchettes

arc 2000

arc 1950

pré st esprit

droset

comborcières

clocheret

aiguille rouge

aiguille rouge

	⏱	pistes	queues	moguls I II III	off-piste I II III
marmottes	3m10 ⛷6 (!)	■ ■	⚒	●	●
bois de l'ours	4m20 ⛷6 (!)	■ ■	⚒	● ●	● ●
lanchettes	7m00 ⛷4	■	⚒		●
st jaques	8m00 ⛷3 (!)	■ ■	⚒⚒⚒	● ●	● ●
varet	7m00 ⛷8	■ ■	⚒⚒⚒	● ●	● ●
plagnettes	7m30 ⛷4	■ ■	⚒⚒⚒⚒		● ●
bosses	5m30 ⛷1	■		● ● ●	●
grand col	10m20 ⛷4	■	⚒⚒⚒		●
aiguille rouge	3m30 ⛷70 (!)	■ ■	⚒⚒⚒⚒	●	●
pré st esprit	13m50 ⛷3	■	⚒		
comborcières	14m40 ⛷3	■	⚒	●	●

ⓘ	
bois de l'ours	this is the quickest way to the the 1800 sector
bosses	often closed
plagnettes	access to the aiguille grive, and the ice grotto
lanchettes	villaroger access
comborcières	arc 1600 access

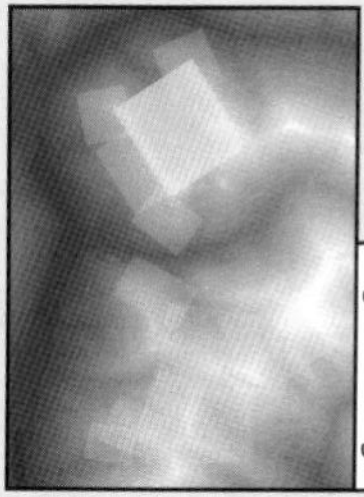

1	les chalets d'arc
2	la crèche
3	au pre gourmand
4	belliou la fumée
5	energy 3000
6	energy 3000

b

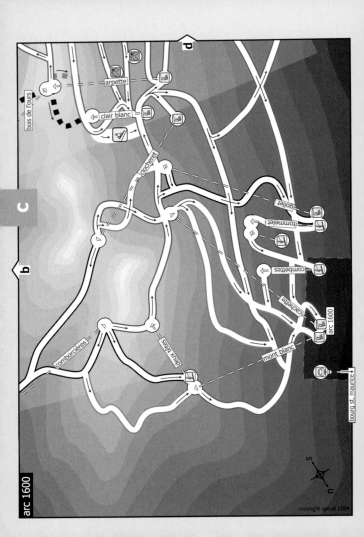

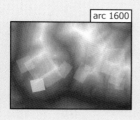

arc 1600

arc 1600

		⏱	pistes	queues	moguls			off-piste		
					I	II	III	I	II	III
mont blanc	🚠3	11m00	▨▨	≋≋					●	
cachette	🚠4	7m20	▨■	≋≋		●		●		
gollet	🚠3	11m20	▨ (i)	≋		●				
combettes	🚡1	3m20	■							
tommelet	🚡1	3m30	■							
deux têtes	🚡1	3m00	▨■	≋≋		●			●	
clocheret	🚠4	4m30	▨■	≋≋≋	●	●	●		●	
clair blanc	🚠2	6m40	▨	≋≋						
arpette	🚠3	10m20	▨■	≋≋ (i)		●	●		●	●

(i) clocheret — aiguille rouge sector access
    arpette — aiguille rouge sector access

(i) clair blanc — snowpark access – the clair blanc will be
    replaced with a new lift in winter 2005-2006

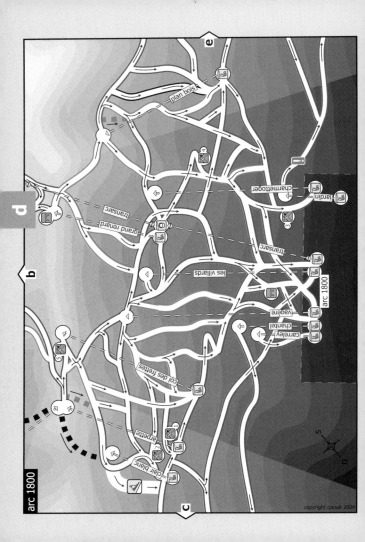

arc 1800

plan bois

charmettoger

jardin

transarc

grand renard

transarc

les villards

arc 1800

vagère

carreley chantel

col des frettes

arpette

clair blanc

copyright ganuk 2004

arc 1800

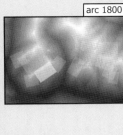

arc 1800

		⏱	pistes	queues	moguls I II III IIII	off-piste I II III IIII
carreley	4	5m00				
chantel	3	8m50				
vagère	6	7m15		(!)		● ●
les villards	4	8m40		🌨		● ● ●
i transarc	🕐15	13m40		🌨		● ●
charmettoger	4	13m20		🌨	●	●
i jardin	4	4m30				
i clair blanc	2	6m40		🌨		●
arpette	3	10m20		■	● ●	● ●
col des frettes	3	9m00		🌨	●	●
i grand renard	3	7m40				
plan bois	4	10m20		🌨	●	●

---

i clair blanc	snowpark access - the clair blanc will be replaced with a new lift in winter 2005-2006
grand renard/transarc	for the aiguille rounge sector it is much faster to take the grand renard than to join the transarc at the mid-station
jardin	there are no pistes leading to this lift

p

1	l'arpette
2	l'altiport
3	l'aiguille grive
4	blanche murée
5	energy 3000

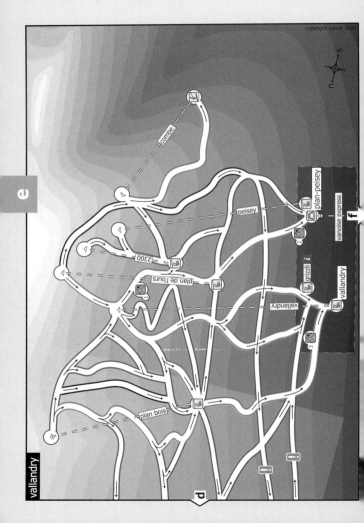

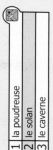

1 la poudreuse
2 le solan
3 le caverne

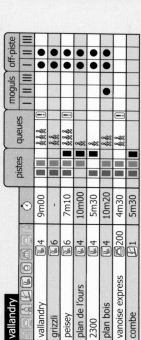

vallandry

		⏱	pistes	queues	moguls I II III IIII	off-piste I II III IIII
vallandry	4	9m00		⚠		● ●
grizzli	6	-				● ●
peisey	6	7m10		⚠		● ●
plan de l'ours	4	10m00				● ●
2300	4	5m30				● ●
plan bois	4	10m20			●	● ●
vanoise express	200	4m30				
combe	1	5m30		⚠		

grizzli — the grizzli chairlift is new in winter 2004

vallandry/plan bois — you can get to arc 1800 from the top of the vallandry chairlift, but the skiing is better accessed by taking the plan bois chairlift

vanoise express — la plagne access

c

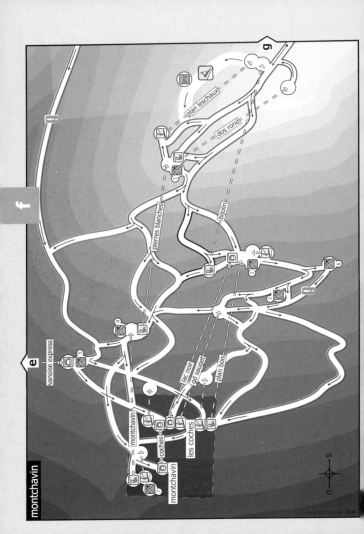

montchavin

vanoise express

plan leschaux

dos rond

pierres blanches

birolin

lac noir

gd saulget

plan bois

montchavin

coches

les coches

montchavin

copyright pistpub 2004

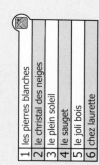

montchavin

montchavin		🕐	pistes	queues	moguls I II III IIII	off-piste I II III IIII
i	montchavin	4	7m20	■ ■	✗✗✗	●	
i	coches	6	3m30	■ ■			
	vanoise express	200	4m30		(!)		
	lac noir	12	6m30	■	✗✗✗		
i	gd sauget	1	6m30	■ ■	✗✗✗		
i	plan bois	2	15m00	■ ■	✗✗		
i	pierres blanches	6	6m00	■ ■	✗✗	●	
i	bijolin	-	-	■	✗✗✗		●
i	dos rond	4	7m20	■	✗✗✗	(!)	●
i	plan leschaux	1	4m00	■	✗		●

i	
coches	pedestrian lift
plan bois	due to be replaced in winter 2005
bijolin	new in winter 2004
plan leschaux	snowpark access
vanoise express	les arcs access

✗	
1	les pierres blanches
2	le christal des neiges
3	le plein soleil
4	le sauget
5	le joli bois
6	chez laurette

f

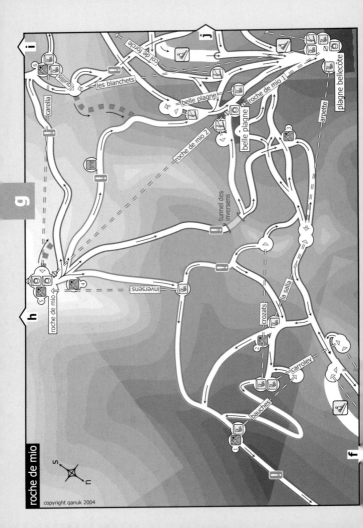

roche de mio

copyright qanuk 2004

les blanchets
col de forcle
belle plagne
roche de mio 1
roche de mio 2
roche de mio
carella
plagne bellecôte
arpette
belle plagne
tunnel des inversens
inversens
la saîla
crozats
carroley
bauches

roche de mio

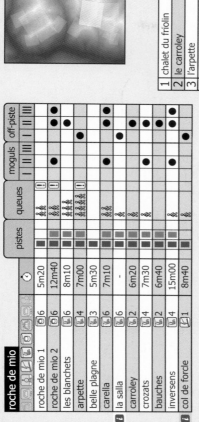

		⏱	pistes	queues	moguls I	moguls II	moguls III	off-piste I	off-piste II	off-piste III
roche de mio 1	6	5m20							●	|||
roche de mio 2	6	12m40				●			●	●
les blanchets	6	8m10								
arpette	4	7m00					●			
belle plagne	3	5m30								
carella	6	7m10				●			●	
la salla	6	-								
carroley	2	6m20							●	
crozats	4	7m30				●			●	
bauches	2	6m40							●	
inversens	4	15m00							●	●
col de force	1	8m40					●			●

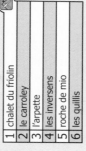

roche de mio

1 chalet du friolin
2 le carroley
3 l'arpette
4 les inversens
5 roche de mio
6 les quillis

col de force — snowpark access
la salla — new lift in winter 2004

9

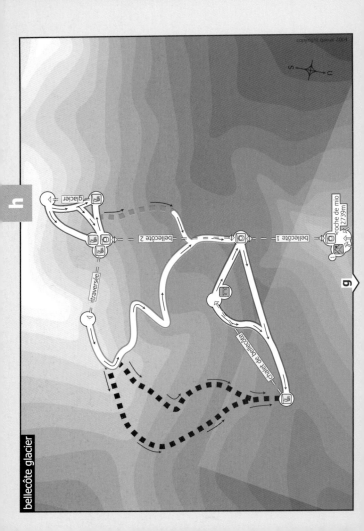

bellecôte glacier

h

g

glacier

traversée

bellecôte 2

bellecôte 1

roche de mio
[2739m]

glacier de bellecôte

copyright ganvar 2004

N
S

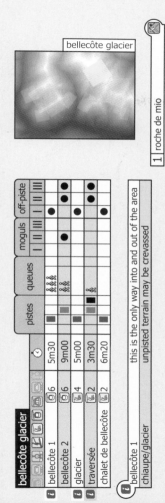

bellecôte glacier

	⏱	pistes	queues	moguls				off-piste		
ℹ bellecôte 1	🚡6	5m30	▰ ≋≋						●	
ℹ bellecôte 2	🚡6	9m00	▰ ≋≋		●				●	
ℹ glacier	🚠4	5m00	▰				●		●	
ℹ traversée	🚠2	3m30	▰ ◼	≋						●
chalet de bellecôte	🚠2	6m20	▰				●			

ℹ bellecôte 1	this is the only way into and out of the area
chiaupe/glacier	unpisted terrain may be crevassed

bellecôte glacier

1 roche de mio

h

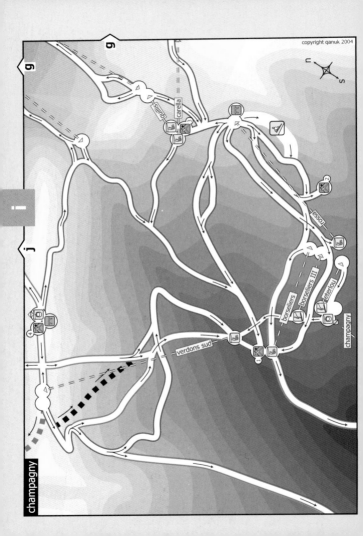

champagny

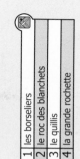

champagny

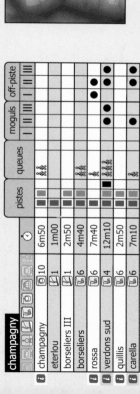

		⏱	pistes	queues	moguls I	II	III	IIII	off-piste I	II	III	IIII
i	champagny	🚠10	6m50	■									
	eterlou	1	1m00	■									
	borseliers III	1	2m50	■	※								
i	borseliers	6	4m40	■									
i	rossa	6	7m40	■	※	●					●	●	
i	verdons sud	4	12m10	■	※	●	●			●	●		
i	quillis	6	2m50	■									
i	carella	6	7m10	■	※			●		●		●	

i	
champagny	return to champagny when the runs down are closed
verdons sud	plagne centre access
rossa	snowpark access
carella	leads to the roche de mio
quillis	belle plagne & plagne bellecôte access

1	les borseliers
2	le roc des blanchets
3	le quillis
4	la grande rochette

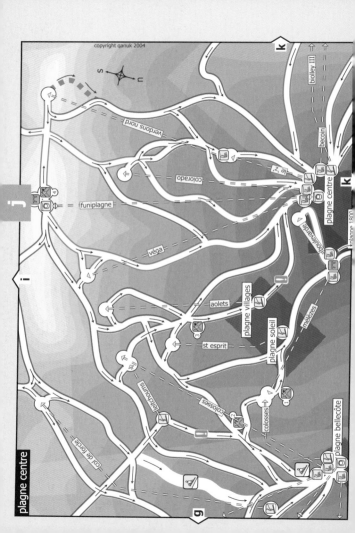

plagne centre

lift		⏱	pistes				queues	moguls I	moguls II	moguls III	off-piste I	off-piste II	off-piste III
funiplagne	12	7m40			■		🚶🚶🚶🚶					●	●
colorado	6	6m00		■	■		🚶🚶					●	
le 'z'	1	3m10		■			🚶						
verdons nord	4	9m50		■	■	■	🚶🚶		●	●		●	
vega	2	11m40		■	■		🚶						
boulevarde	4	4m00	■										
mélèzes	4	8m10		■			🚶					●	
leitchoums	1	4m30		■								●	
aolets	1	4m50		■			🚶					●	
st esprit	1	4m00		■									
colosses	4	7m30		■			🚶🚶🚶					●	
colosses	1	4m00		■			🚶					●	
col de force	1	8m40		■			🚶				●		

plagne centre

colorado/le 'z' & verdons nord	alternative routes to champagny if the funiplagne is busy
mélèzes	the quickest link to plagne bellecote
vega	the vega is very slow
col de force	snowpark access

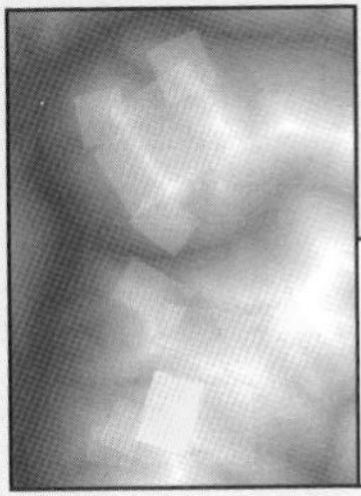

1	le dou de praz
2	chalet de la trieuse
3	la bergerie
4	la grande rochette

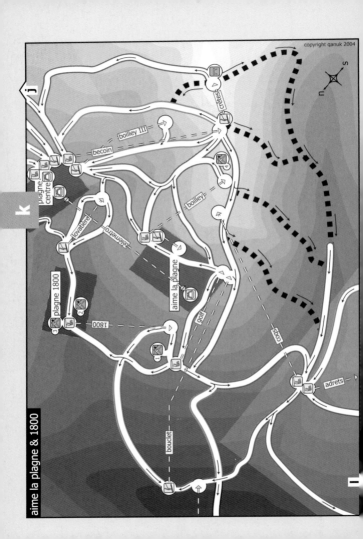

aime la plagne & 1800

copyright qanuk 2004

aime la plagne & 1800

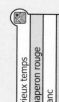
aime la plagne & 1800

		⏱	pistes	queues	moguls I II III	off-piste I II III
télémetro	🚡40	5m40				
golf	4	5m40		⚡		I
biolley	4	7m00	■	⚡	●	● ≡
becoin	4	9m10	■	⚡	● ●	● ● ≡
biolley III	1	3m30	■	⚡		
crêtes	1	2m00	■		●	● I
coqs	4	11m00	■	⚡	● ●	● ● ≡
lovatière	1	2m40				
1800	4	5m40	■	⚡		
bouclet	1	6m40				● I

ℹ		
télémetro	pedestrian lift	
bouclet	téléski difficile	
crêtes	téléski difficile	

ℹ	
1	aux bon vieux temps
2	le petit chaperon rouge
3	la loup blanc
4	le biollet

k

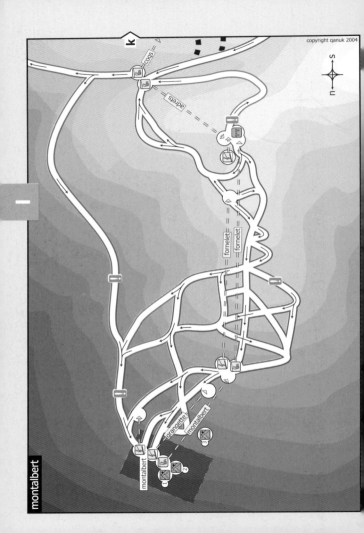

montalbert

copyright qanuk 2004

montalbert

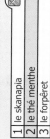

montalbert

			pistes	queues	moguls I II III IIII IIIII	off-piste I II III IIII	
montalbert	🚡4	3m30	▪ ▪				
grangette	🚡1	3m30	▪ ▪ ▪	✕			
fornelet	🚡4	12m30	▪ ▪ ▪			●	
fornelet	🚡1	6m20	▪ ▪ ▪ ▪	✕			
adrets	🚡4	6m00	▪ ▪ ▪ ▪	✕		●	

| grangette | closed in late season |
| fornelet draglift | closed in late season |

◇ ski area key

les arcs

a - villaroger
b - aiguille rouge
c - arc 1600
d - arc 1800
e - vallandry

la plagne

f - montchavin
g - roche de mio
h - bellecôte glacier
i - champagny
j - plagne centre
k - aime la plagne & 1800
l - montalbert

the circle indicates the page orientation
of the individual ski maps - the arrow
points towards the top of the page